"For those numbed by the relentless polarization of this era, *Beauty and Resistance* is a stirring call to action. We have enough authors who tell us how we can change the world, but Jonathan Walton adds something else: a rule of life for embracing beauty and rest as well as resistance. At the core of Walton's story is a refreshing honesty, vulnerability, and a welcome belief that resistance and beauty can not only coexist but thrive together."

John Blake, CNN editor and author of *More Than I Imagined*

"In *Beauty and Resistance*, Jonathan Walton offers a pastorally wise and prophetically grounded invitation to follow Jesus into rhythms of rest, resistance, and renewal. In a world burdened by injustice and despair, Walton guides us toward a sustainable activism—one rooted not in urgency or outrage but in the life-giving presence of the triune God."

Caleb E. Campbell, author of *Disarming Leviathan*

"In *Beauty and Resistance*, Jonathan Walton casts a holistic vision of life in the kingdom of God—a kingdom that contrasts and upends the kingdoms and idols of this world. He pairs this vision with much-needed emphasis on sustainable emotional and spiritual formation to fuel a vibrant life of Christian justice. The church desperately needs this pairing of prophetic witness and sustainable spirituality, and Walton's stories can help us!"

Jason Jensen, vice president of spiritual foundations for InterVarsity Christian Fellowship/USA and author of *Formed to Lead*

"Jonathan Walton embodies a lived gospel of hope and justice, guiding generations of students. If you are looking for a vital, restorative rhythm for sustainable justice rooted in spiritual renewal and deep engagement, this is your guide!"

Sandra Maria Van Opstal, founder of Chasing Justice and author of *The Next Worship*

BEAUTY +
RESISTANCE

spiritual rhythms for formation and repair

JONATHAN P.
WALTON

ivp

An imprint of InterVarsity Press
Downers Grove, Illinois

InterVarsity Press
P.O. Box 1400 | Downers Grove, IL 60515-1426
ivpress.com | email@ivpress.com

InterVarsity Press® is the publishing division of InterVarsity Christian Fellowship/USA®. For more information, visit intervarsity.org.

All Scripture quotations, unless otherwise indicated, are taken from The Holy Bible, New International Version®, NIV®. Copyright © 1973, 1978, 1984, 2011 by Biblica, Inc.™ Used by permission of Zondervan. All rights reserved worldwide. www.zondervan.com. The "NIV" and "New International Version" are trademarks registered in the United States Patent and Trademark Office by Biblica, Inc.™

Published in association with Gardner Literary.

While any stories in this book are true, some names and identifying information may have been changed to protect the privacy of individuals.

The publisher cannot verify the accuracy or functionality of website URLs used in this book beyond the date of publication.

Cover design: Faceout Studio
Interior design: Daniel van Loon
Images: © Yevhenii via Adobe Stock, © Nikola via Adobe Stock

ISBN 978-1-5140-1228-4 (print) | ISBN 978-1-5140-1229-1 (digital)

Printed in the United States of America ∞

Library of Congress Cataloging-in-Publication Data
A catalog record for this book is available from the Library of Congress.

31 30 29 28 27 26 25 | 12 11 10 9 8 7 6 5 4 3 2 1

To Priscilla, Maia, and Everest.

You are accepted. God is not ashamed of you.

You are his and he is yours.

You are children of the Most High God.

And I am too.

The Son is the image of the invisible God, the firstborn over all creation. For in him all things were created: things in heaven and on earth, visible and invisible, whether thrones or powers or rulers or authorities; all things have been created through him and for him. He is before all things, and in him all things hold together.

COLOSSIANS 1:15-17

Suppose one of you wants to build a tower. Won't you first sit down and estimate the cost to see if you have enough money to complete it? For if you lay the foundation and are not able to finish it, everyone who sees it will ridicule you, saying, "This person began to build and wasn't able to finish."

JESUS (LUKE 14:28-30)

CONTENTS

INTRODUCTION

Pride is often more visible in others,
but its grip is strongest on ourselves.

UNKNOWN

In early 2023, I wept in the car from anxiety one Friday afternoon. I was afraid of losing my job. *This isn't supposed to happen to me*, I thought. As an employee of a Christian ministry responsible for raising my own salary and benefits, I thought, *Seriously, how is this happening to me?* I'm a good employee and my last performance review had no hangups. I was confused, sad, and disappointed.

And then, to my surprise, I said to myself—and kind of to God—"I'm a good Christian. I don't deserve this."

Later that year I woke up on a Tuesday morning and filled the toilet with red pee. Half asleep, I tried to remember if something had been in the toilet before I started. I looked down and looked away, looked down and looked away, trying to remember what I'd eaten or drunk that might do this. I took pictures to text my doctor friends and sat in a urologist's office later that week. I had no idea what was happening to me. Ultimately, they didn't either. Again I asked God, "Why?"

I was stressed, anxious, and not doing well. The challenges seemed to come all at once. My wife, Priscilla, ruptured her Achilles tendon, leaving her bedridden for forty-two days, save for assisted showers and physical therapy. I responded the only respectable way I knew how: suck it up and keep going. Activate Super Jonathan! Pickup and drop-off for both kids; meal prep for each week; all the laundry, garbage, and compost; doctors' appointments and late nights; tax prep and budgeting—all of this I would handle perfectly.

The problem is, I'm not superhuman and no one was asking me to be. But I convinced myself otherwise. Anything less and I would be a failure. Predictably, I came up short and made poor decisions.

Contrary to what Priscilla and I had agreed to at the time, I frequently told my kids they could do activities that were not in our budget because I didn't want to disappoint them. I told my eldest she could do gymnastics and a local science camp in the summer. And then I had to go back and tell her I'd made a mistake. She looked up at me and said, "It's okay, Baba."

But her face said I'd broken a promise. I knew that face. It was the same one I gave my dad when he said he was coming to church and didn't show up, when he was going to buy a birthday present and didn't, or when he promised my mom he would pay a bill but I came up with the money instead. So when I saw her see me, I was gutted. I could not live with myself if I created the same uncertain, chaotic home I'd grown up in.

From the opposite side of our white picket fence, things looked dreamy. I was married with two kids, a dog, and a home in New York City. I was respected by my peers, and friends and colleagues looked up to me. But I believed the opposite of what I prayed with my daughters every night. I had taught them to say, "I am accepted. God is not ashamed of me. I am his and he is mine. I am a child of God."

I lived as if the opposite were true. I believed God loved me only if I did what he said, never questioned him, and refused help until I'd exhausted my own strength. With my mind I claimed God's love, but in my heart that love never felt secure, like my status as God's child could be revoked at any point.

On the outside I was certain. On the inside I was unstable. I felt guilty for not speaking up more about racial injustice and ashamed for not doing more about climate change. I policed myself, seeing the surveillance footage of my own life, holding up each part and asking, *What would people think?*

Often I found myself completely spent in the afternoons working from home when Alexa blared from the counter to snap me back to the tasks at hand. This day was no different.

The timer I'd set went off and it was time to go and pick up my youngest from school. I had thirteen minutes to make a thirteen-minute trip and I did not have on my shoes yet.

I moved quickly to get out the door but I was stuck. I was stuck in my head feeling the pressure of a high mortgage, high energy costs, and expensive activities that promised to put my kids on the path to success. Stuck in my own sense of inadequacy. If this was the dream, why did I feel like a man in the crowd listening to Denzel Washington as Malcolm X— like I'd been had, took, hoodwinked, bamboozled?

I called my younger brother Nathan to ask for advice. He happens to be a pastor, exceptionally thoughtful, and the same Enneagram and Myers-Briggs personality type as me. We are both Enneagram Threes and INTJs. He is busy but always answers the phone as if nothing else is happening. I appreciate that about him.

I laid my situation out for him, some of which he already knew. There was a gap between the money I wanted to make to feel a sense of worth and the money I was making right now. Bigger, though, was the gap between who I was and who I wanted to be for myself and my family. I feared that if I didn't change anything, our family would be stuck with my best, which was less than what was necessary. We would be on the gotta-pay-our-bills treadmill indefinitely. I felt trapped and thought working harder was the way out.

"You can do that if you want to be single," Nathan said to me bluntly with a chuckle.

If I wanted to make money to maintain our lifestyle, perhaps my lifestyle was the problem. He knew Priscilla and I had worked to prioritize marriage and parenting and created a rule of life that mirrored our hopes and dreams. I was reminded of what a pastor had said to us four years earlier when we'd moved to this home, that it seemed to be against our "universe of values." I started to wonder if he was on to something. Years back I would have dismissed both of them and found a wise person who would validate what I wanted to do. But now I had structures to liberate me from the rigid, unchecked person I'd been before, and I sensed they were right.

I was overworked and overwhelmed, and I lacked a regular sleep schedule. I wanted to live differently, but I was telling myself I couldn't. I was Jonathan Walton. Pride is a sin that can be most deceiving. I should have known it was a problem when I started to refer to myself in the third person when reflecting on my own limitations.

All my vulnerabilities felt exposed, but most days I was in denial that I had any.

I know what it is to white-knuckle myself through work and activism. A tree is recognized by the fruit that it bears, and the seeds I'd sown produced distance, not intimacy. They prioritized correction over connection with people. The fruit of those labors were not fruits of the Spirit.

I don't want to live that way anymore. I must sow different seeds to reap different fruit.

Every day I try to grow and change, embracing the God-given limits of my humanity through life-giving rhythms that remind me Jesus is the Messiah—not me.

We must take ownership over care for ourselves and those we love, as well as the vulnerable we care for with whatever abundance we are blessed to have. We must also choose vulnerability, asking for and receiving care for ourselves. This is life in good tension, and it is not a dismissal of responsibility or sign of weakness. Understanding what is actually happening and taking responsibility is a crucial part of living out the Great Commission and the Great Commandments. When this faith becomes profound action, it leads to flourishing and fruitfulness that is accessible to us every day and should be evident to the world around us.

As of writing this sentence, I have used the Peloton at least once a week for 108 weeks straight and have a streak of twenty-three days. I realized I couldn't love my neighbor well if I didn't love myself. And part of loving me was stretching so my back wasn't tight. I have to ride the bike so I can walk without stiffness. I lift weights so I can play with my kids. Most of all I use meditations to slow down, de-stress, and stay grounded. All of these things help me be present to myself, God, and others in an intimate way that I wasn't initially open to but now can't live without.

I knew my pace of life was unsustainable, and now I can admit it. I also knew that God made me good and limits are gifts, and now I want to live that way. I am learning to embrace my humanity, and that includes the truth that I can't change everything overnight. My children need health insurance, and the mortgage is due whether I am anxious or content about my employer. If my youngest wakes up with a fever, I'll be in bed with her at night and at urgent care with her in the morning. There will be recorded incidents of police brutality, corruption, greed, and war. And I will be left searching for the words and work of God in it all.

But as Princess Anna of Arendelle sang in *Frozen II*, I can "do the next right thing." If I experience a setback, struggle, and suffering, I can slow down, pivot, and live out of my deepest values, not my deepest wounds or whims. I can feel my feelings and live in reality without anger, sadness, or anxiety defining everything around me.

These rhythms are not necessary just in times of crisis or response to an emergency, only to be used like an ax behind glass or a spiritual spare tire when my life is on fire or my soul has a flat. They are the ebb and flow of my very existence, because the abundant beauty of God and the reality that his love and justice have not yet come to all of creation are constant and concurrent.

I may not get eight hours of sleep because my kids don't go down easily, but I don't need to practice revenge bedtime procrastination. Spending forty-five minutes on my phone grasping for a sense of agency and control over my time is not helping me. I may not have my dream job or forever home, but I'm still worthy of joy, can practice gratitude, and am able to give and receive love and celebrate others' success.

When I hear about governors exploiting immigrants' vulnerability and dropping them off in cities of political rivals, I don't have to be consumed by rage and disbelief and scroll and share incessantly. I don't have to check out, disengage from current events, or diminish the suffering of people nearby and worldwide. I can learn about what's happening, lament the tragedy, and confess my ignorance and my complicity. Then I can listen for how God would want me to partner with him and others to follow the Jesus of love and justice into discerned, deliberate action.

The same is true of every mass shooting, natural disaster, genocide, and population displacement. I can pray to the God who made everything, holds it all together, and is making all things new. I can assess my gifts and limits and collaborate as faithfully as I am able with God in light of his absolute power, abundant provision, infinite knowledge, and presence everywhere. All of this and more I will never do perfectly. But if I allow God to perfect me, then I will avail myself of the beauty available to me and be able to resist the individual, intimate, interpersonal, institutional, and ideological ways his shalom is disrupted. My actions will flow from my identity and I can truly be a human being, not a human doing.

The core issue was that I had been drawn more to resistance than to beauty, even though God was calling me to embrace both in abundance.

So I began taking baby steps.

I began mourning, rejoicing, resting, and working—all at once. It felt full, hard, and delightful. There was beauty and resistance. Something deep was shifting.

THE SCAFFOLDING

In construction, scaffolding is a temporary structure to support a building while it is being built or repaired. These metal poles, wooden planks, and steel nuts and bolts are as essential as the people and materials they hold up. Scaffolding is also a term used in education referring to a teaching method that provides supportive structures for students as they learn new concepts and master new skills. Just like with a building, when the supports are removed, a student should stand on their own and demonstrate proficiency. In both contexts, the primary goal of scaffolding is to provide necessary support until the person or building can stand and succeed independently.

I needed a structure to support and sustain me as God worked in me to become the person he'd called me to be. I required a system that ensured I had the inner strength, courage, and wisdom to face both joys and challenges. It was not just about learning new information or mastering new skills. I needed to be transformed and continually renewed. Ephesians 2:10 says, "We are God's handiwork, created in Christ Jesus to do good works, which God prepared in advance for us to do."

I needed rhythms that helped me stay attuned to the voice of our Maker, because there was an abundance of riches from heaven that the apostle Paul prayed I would receive. Paul said:

> For this reason I kneel before the Father, from whom every family in heaven and on earth derives its name. I pray that out of his glorious riches he may strengthen you with power through his Spirit in your inner being, so that Christ may dwell in your hearts through faith. And I pray that you, being rooted and established in love, may have power, together with all the Lord's holy people, to grasp how wide and long and high and deep is the love of Christ, and to know this love that surpasses knowledge—that you may be filled to the measure of all the fullness of God. (Ephesians 3:14-19)

If God is truly sovereign, Christ is the Messiah, and the Spirit created order from chaos, then the Master Teacher and Master Builder have to provide the scaffolding I need on this side of eternity.

After this reckoning and realization, I could begin the walk toward becoming fully present to the beauty God provides and the resistance he calls me to. Jesus called me to a rule of life organized not just around lamenting or rejoicing but around both in full measure, along with rest and work. He called me to four practices: rest, restoration, resistance, and repetition. And I believe he is calling you too. Not just because we live in a particularly difficult time where special practices and disciplines are needed, but because abundant reception of and involvement in beauty and resistance are marks of a life lived with God.

A rule of life is a set of intentional practices that support long-term, prayerful growth. Jesus calls us to be disciples, not interns or employees. Traditionally, a rule of life is compared to a trellis, which supports plants like cucumbers or tomatoes, allowing them to grow upward and bear fruit, and it is practiced in community. In the same way, I need structure to strengthen my relationship with God and sustain my work in community with others. I am a human being, not a human doing, and this truth applies to everyone.

My goal is not to chase fleeting moments of fulfillment or swing between highs and lows. Instead, I seek steady growth through deliverance and discipleship, with regular time for work, rest, play, reflection, delight, and service.

AN INVITATION

I believe that a desire for personal and social renewal and shalom is something you and I have in common. Humanity was made out of love for love, justice, and shalom—peace between all relationships. In fleeting moments of deep reflection, the key change of a gospel song, or even an unexpected TikTok or Instagram reel that just hits you, I know you feel it too.

If history and Scripture offer any wisdom, movements for love and justice are difficult to sustain. Many, including myself, desire change but don't have the inner lives to do anything sustainable and long term about it. And we often lack the communal ties to keep us going when things get tough.

I often find myself staving off a familiar pattern when I am sparked to seek some sort of change but hit a snag. I cope, medicate, and crash just to start the cycle all over again when the spark comes and adversity hits back. And so I don't build anything new or truly change even though I say I want something different. I start something but just can't keep it up. My fear of change, anxiety about the future, and need to survive press me into isolation and hopelessness or logic and practicality as the next way to go. I suspect the same is true for you.

Our current habits of engaging with the world might help us cope in the moment but sink us for the long term. I'm looking at you, Zillow browsing, Netflix watching, and a few drinks too many. But when we rely on these habits alone, they often move us away from imagining a new way forward. Why? The reality is, change often feels complicated, difficult, and impossible. Fortunately, Jesus is not intimidated by any of this, and the gospel speaks eternal wisdom to us today.

Jesus' first sermon in Luke 4 invited all the listeners to imagine a world where the blind could see, the lame could walk, and the enslaved were set free. He regularly pulled the disciples and all who were observing them toward embodying the wholeness meant for each person present. And I am convinced he desires the same for us. This would have been foolishness at worst and fulfillment of prophecy at best to those listening. It was the latter, and it was precisely what all of those gathered needed to hear in the midst of their suffering, sickness, and compromises for survival. We need that too.

Instead of an algorithm that keeps us distracted by entertainment or outrage, or companies concerned only with our consumption and engagement, we must meet the Jesus birthed by a Nazarene teenager in the midst of Roman occupation. We must take up our crosses, deny false selves, and follow him like two fishermen, a tax collector, and a local activist did. And we must do it every day, week, month, season, and year, individually and in community, to receive and reflect the shalom God intended.

Let us be scaffolded by God and one another for beauty and resistance, because it is what the Father created us for and who he has made us to be.

THE RECKONING

1

For two decades, I accepted that my life would be defined by resistance. My conscious norm was pain, disappointment, and struggle. Nothing felt easy, and the substance of my life obscured the beauty around me. So much so that I stopped looking for beauty altogether.

This perspective is logical, given where I come from. I think of my great-grandfather, who around 1900 asked a White man to buy land for him because the law wouldn't let him purchase it himself. The notion that my great-grandfather could raise a family, make a living, and own land in the heart of southern Virginia—where lynchings were not uncommon, the KKK was active, and Black codes were in place—was audacious.[1] How did my great-grandfather, a grown man, fashion himself into a boy and back again? He had to walk up and ask for that land, perhaps eyes down and hat off in a context that defined him as less than human. He probably planned it for some time, or he was so fluent in White supremacy and well-versed in protecting the comfort of the powerful that he knew how to approach the situation instinctively. I'm not sure. But he would have had to walk home from that scenario of subservience to be a husband and father in his own household. Lord have mercy.

How often have I felt that in my own life?

I think of my mother, who was born on that land purchased by someone else for her grandfather. She grew up in Brodnax, Virginia, where she was stared at—with *the* stare—as she left segregated East End High School in 1969 to attend integrated Park View High School in 1970.[2] The "why are you here?" stare. The "you don't belong here" stare. The stare that dared you to say anything about being followed around the store or the scoreboard not changing when *you people* scored during an integrated basketball game. She was one of the millions of Ruby Bridges who didn't have a documentary, podcast, or movie made about her but who carried the pain in her bones of that same narrative journey.

I wish the famous stories didn't resonate as normal. And I understand the efforts to reframe the ability to struggle and overcome as grit, tenacity, and resilience. At the same time, the seeds of violence—enslavement, Jim Crow, police brutality, redlining, patriarchy—that made my mom's life so hard never needed to be planted in the first place.

I know the de-formation and re-formation process. I was de-formed by society to fit into socially acceptable boxes for years and re-formed elsewhere if those around me were conscious of the tools necessary for freedom and growth;

often, though, it was just another box to ensure my safety and survival.

That's what "the talk" is all about. Black folks need to know the boxes that are safe to be in when interacting with law enforcement.

Millions of White Americans have learned about the discussion Black American parents and other parents of color give our children about how to respond to the police. In the wake of the murders of Ahmaud Arbery, Breonna Taylor, and George Floyd, a conversation that normally happens on the margins suddenly became a mainstream subject on news outlets across the political, social, and economic spectrum.

Ahmaud Arbery was killed in Brunswick, Georgia, by a group of White men who believed him to be a burglar when he was out for an afternoon jog on February 23, 2020. Shortly after this, Breonna Taylor was shot while sleeping in her bed on March 13, 2020, in Louisville, Kentucky, during the execution of a "no-knock warrant." This controversial practice allows officers to go into a residence without announcing themselves or giving any advance notice. She was shot six times. Later, on May 25, 2020, George Floyd was killed in Minneapolis after an officer kneeled on his neck for nearly ten minutes while a crowd watched in horror.

These are the stories most people know about. But *The Guardian* reports that in the United States, police killed 1,152 people in 2020.[3] That is more than three people per day.

Suddenly the conversations I and many others have with our children in private were streaming on social media, discussed by pundits on Fox News and CNN, and published in books that pushed people deeper into their rabbit holes and echo chambers.

I thought this was all the stuff of life. Life was marked by pain, painted by struggle, and defined by resistance. To live was to push emotions down, hold tears back, and harden our hearts in order to brave a society that doesn't want us to be part of it—though it does want our labor. I didn't know how to talk to my kids about the richness of our heritage and ethnic identity. I couldn't describe the beauty of our history, which can feel miraculous given the sheer level of disadvantage and violence that Black, Indigenous, and other people of color have faced over the last five hundred years, along with the trauma that entails. I knew the gospel but I needed the liberated wisdom of the good news.

THE CROSS WITH NO RESURRECTION

When I decided to follow Jesus, this didn't change much. In the context of my college fellowship, I internalized the idea that to be faithful was to be crucified, knowing resurrection was coming but not soon or in full. I had to be strong, wait on the Lord, and take up my cross. To be a Christian was to resist the evil in the world and the evil in myself. Looking back, I realize that my life did not lack beauty—I just couldn't see it.

So I embraced the resistance. Or at least a version of it. I worked for money, for justice, and sometimes for both, but I always stayed busy. For far too long, if I caught a glimpse of beauty, I refused to embrace it because I didn't have a historical, theological, or emotional category for it. Delight was temporary and therefore unproductive, so it was not worth my time. I tried to keep an even keel, never growing too excited, angry, or sad, and so my spectrum of emotions narrowed. I built a résumé on my own efforts and righteousness that I asked Jesus to bless and people to like. And since people liked me, I thought Jesus blessed it. My wife and others sounded alarms, but I was unable to respond meaningfully to their invitations to be different or warnings to get off the path.

When I started therapy in 2013, I was warned to not burn out, to be present to those around me, and to truly allow my feelings to rise up and be made known. It was a struggle. I distinctly remember in group therapy being asked questions and responding with canned Sunday school answers. They almost laughed me out of the room. These men and women had seen the good Christian guy before and were not interested in a sermon or Bible study. They wanted to get to know me. And not just what I was passionate about, but me as a person. And I didn't know where to start.

I remember multiple times sitting down with the family of my wife, Priscilla, when we first started dating. They, too, wanted to get to know me. They didn't want to hear where I went to college, what books I had written, or where I worked. They wanted to know about my family, what it was like to grow up in Brodnax, and what my hopes and dreams were for the future—independent of my ambitions.

In my head I thought, why would I do that? If I shared my feelings and didn't get the reaction I wanted, I could be hurt again. I could talk about the gospel songs that held our house together and the Motown ones that blew it apart. And then I'd have to explain what gospel music is and who the Temptations are. What would be the point? I had no interest in discussing the moments in my childhood when I longed for connection and was often met with confusion, silence, disgust, or rejection. I could not bear the weight of that disappointment.

Eventually I came to realize that the point was connection, relationship, and love. I could feel disappointed and share how, why, and make requests. I could not love someone I was trying to control or manipulate, and I could receive love even amid conflict. I was just plain lovable, and so was everyone around me. We are all worthy of being known. This was a slippery truth—one I am still trying to hold on to.

While I was trying to do the deep work of healing, the breadth of God's love seemed to expand. My growing awareness of and resistance to police violence intensified this reality for me. Moreover, the ramp-up to the 2020 election season was tumultuous, the Covid-19 pandemic was debilitating, and hate crimes against Asian Americans were widespread. Donald Trump was unapologetically racist and sexist, and his first presidential term was chaotic, cruel, and endorsed by many who claimed to follow Jesus around me.

Adam Serwer's 2018 essay in *The Atlantic*, "The Cruelty Is the Point," makes a clear and compelling argument. Serwer identifies the disturbing reality communities of color, women, the poor, Muslims, the disabled, immigrants, and LGBTQIA+ people found themselves in during Trump's election campaigns and presidency. Trump filled hours of media time with speeches that mocked, condemned, and threatened vulnerable communities, explaining who you "should" hate and why.[4]

For example, Serwer points out the courageous testimony of Christine Blasey-Ford, who came forward with her story of past sexual assault perpetrated by then–Supreme Court nominee Brett Kavanaugh. Before a panel of United States senators, she recounted her experience with steadfast clarity. When questioned by Democratic Senator Patrick Leahy, who asked her to recount her assault, she described the "uproarious laughter" of her attackers as they fumbled with her clothing. She named this disturbing detail of her ordeal, and then Trump amplified it days later. At a rally he ridiculed her before thousands of people, who laughed alongside him.[5]

Serwer notes, "The president's mocking of her testimony renders all sexual-assault survivors collateral damage. Anyone afraid of coming forward, afraid that she would not be believed, can now look to the president to see her fears realized."

This effect stretched across marginalized groups when Trump encouraged police abuse as they laughed in the background and made fun of *New York Times* reporter Serg Kovalesky, who has a congenital joint condition that causes his arms to remain in a bent position.[6] Perhaps most devastating was when Trump called SARS-CoV-2 "the China virus," which precipitated a terrible rise in violence against the Asian diaspora here in the United States.[7] Trump separated families at the border, revoked protections for undocumented immigrants brought to the United States as children, and attacked NFL players for protesting.[8]

These were perilous, destabilizing times. They still are.

But during the heights of unrest, I was not posting on social media or organizing prayer meetings and protests. I was not mobilizing leaders, pressing for reforms, or leveraging my platform to turn more attention to these tragedies. I was a Black man holding my newborn Black Chinese Korean American daughter in the wake of Ahmaud Arbery's slaying, unprepared for the Atlanta spa shooting that happened less than a year later, and washing packages to protect us from the pandemic.[9] I was on sabbatical from what I thought my purpose was. Then, I went on paternity leave and remained off social media and organizing for twelve months.

Why? Because I'd completely burned out.

Before the advent of Covid-19 and the birth of my second daughter, I checked my phone compulsively. I felt compelled to respond to every to comment and monitor likes, shares, and follows because I conflated engagement online with God's favor and success. Meanwhile, my life was on fire. Prior to my sabbatical and the birth of my daughter, I burned the candle at both ends and in the middle in pursuit of a false identity I chased relentlessly with every waking hour. I sat for hours in Grand Central Station writing, often until the wee hours of the morning. Historically, I wrote poetry, but after Michael Brown was killed in Ferguson, Missouri, in 2014, I chose prose.

IN DESPERATE NEED OF A NEW STORY

For five years, the story I'd told myself was that if I just wrote the right words, perhaps Christians worshiping Trump would come to their senses. If I just had the right caption on a photo on Instagram or wrote the right thing for HuffPost, light would crack through the fog and people would see the counterfeit kingdom of God that America is. I poured my heart out in essays and spent my voice on speaking. I wrote, read, and reshared articles, and watched documentaries using the free Wi-Fi in Vanderbilt Hall, trying to think through what resources and experiences might lead students from Cooper Union to take jobs that created life instead of going to work for weapons manufacturers. Could I write the essay that made Black Lives Matter to police and end the constant stream of brutality? I could and I would, I thought.

In hindsight, it's easy to see what I was doing. Part of my efforts fed a hunger for external validation that hadn't appeared out of nowhere. It was created inside me before kindergarten, tied to a void, an absence of affirmation that my father never filled and an anti-Black society exacerbated within me. I followed my momma's prompting to "not be like my dad" and took White society's invitation to be a good one. When I heard "be a good one," it was a warning, insult, and invitation. A warning because to not be a good one could mean lynching or the loss of a job opportunity, scholarship, home loan, favor, or some other leg up on the ladder of racial hierarchy. It was an insult because it lands like a socially acceptable way to say *good n*****. And an invitation because if I did perform what was asked of me, then my life could be materially and experientially easier.

I heard the warning, felt the insult, and took the invitation. I set out to fashion myself into a model of the men I saw on the ABC Friday night lineup through academic and then economic success. I would live out all of the prayers and prophecies prayed over me every time a church mother realized I shared a birthday with Martin Luther King Jr.— January 15.

And then one day during marriage counseling, Priscilla looked up at me and said, "I'm just not going to try any more. I've been chasing you for too long." This was not our first session and it wouldn't be our last, but her words hung in the air like heavy fog in that second-floor office. The counselor didn't speak, and I didn't know what to say. I had created an environment where she was the gatekeeper. We were not collaborators. In my mind, we were opposing forces.

I would say things like, "Is it okay if I go and speak at this event?" or "Can I write an article for them?" I set her up as the villain and therefore the one to blame. If I did not want to be my dad, it was clear that she did not want to be my mom saying yes or no to a manchild who was unwilling to set and hold his own boundaries, determine priorities, or make plans.

I heard her desperation and felt her invisibility. She made my choice clear: I could live as though I were single, pursuing fame, adoration, and impact. Or I could choose to be significant to the ones with whom I shared the intimacies of life and build a life with them.

I chose the latter.

These and other conversations prompted me to make changes. During my sabbatical and paternity leave in 2019 and 2020, I began seeing two spiritual directors a month and a therapist every week, and I participated in group therapy every Monday night. One evening I was sitting in a room with a candle when one of my spiritual directors,

Kimberly, prompted me to go to a place I had never been by asking a question I had never heard: "Jonathan, if God was your only audience, would that be enough?"

The Sunday school answer is yes, but if I'd said that I would have been lying. So I told her the honest truth: "No." When I admitted that, something split inside me and my head began to ache like never before. Yes, there was much good fruit from all the work I was doing. God was gracious and faithful. But no amount of effective activism and social validation could replace what God offered me simply for being his kid, made in his image to flourish, work, steward, and create. No amount of activity and affirmation could bear the weight of my identity. He alone is and should be my all in all. That truth broke into me at that moment, but I wasn't able to grasp that reality until I took the time to hold my own children closer than my vice of goodness.

FROZEN II AND HOMEMADE PIZZA

I had no idea that faithfulness meant being present to cooing, laughing, and fort building while explaining to my eldest daughter the depiction of reparations, decolonization, and ethnic reconciliation in Disney's *Frozen II* over homemade pizza on our weekly movie nights. I didn't see activism or the destruction of oppressive narratives in my household as valuable as it was in the streets, behind podiums, or from the pulpit. But now I know talks across cups of hot chocolate in our kitchen can be as challenging, formative, and fruitful as those in the four walls of a church or backstage at a conference.

I learned from taking care of my daughters that we could sing "Let It Go" from Disney's *Frozen* at the top of our lungs and lament the deaths of parents while thinking about what it means to be young women in a world where patriarchy reigns. We could celebrate the joy of siblings, friendship, and imagination while contemplating loss, grief, change, and loneliness, because being different is hard. "Do You Want to Build a Snowman?" and Olaf's coming to be were all the things I didn't know I needed and everything I wanted and wished for with my two daughters.

I don't want to spoil this for you because I believe you must watch *Frozen II*, but you must know that Elsa and Anna come from a multiethnic heritage. Their father is royalty from Arendelle and their mother is Northuldra, an indigenous tribe being colonized and exploited by the citizens of Arendelle. Elsa hears voices calling her to a mysterious forest, and when she makes her way in with her magic, Anna and her faithful friends follow. Shortly after some crucial explaining by Olaf, which includes stellar voiceover skills by award-winning actor Josh Gad, Elsa and Anna are sung into their new family. My eyes fill with tears every time. There is so much beauty.

Later in the film (spoiler alert!), when the lies of the colonial power are unearthed, Anna proclaims in an act of liberative reparation that they must destroy the dam used to starve the People of the Sun. The lie is a curse keeping the two worlds separate. Once it is exposed, the dam destroyed, and the water allowed to flow, the people are reconciled. Those in power thought their lives would be destroyed if the dam were to fall, but instead there is flourishing for all people. Beauty is the fruit of their resistance. And resistance is the result of their encounter with beauty. *Lord, have mercy.*

I cry every time Elsa's hands are taken by her ancestors and they begin to sing. I didn't pray with my mom at home until I was twenty years old, but in my little church, the songs bound us together. I sing to, for, and—now that they're older—with my girls every day. I want our songs to be on their hearts. I also pray with them original liturgies I wrote for them before they go to sleep or leave our home. Every night we say:

> *I am accepted.*
> *God is not ashamed of me.*
> *I am his and he is mine.*
> *I am a child of the Most High God.*

What I didn't realize when I wrote that prayer was that it was my own core longing. When our family says it together, there is profound beauty and resistance with each sentence. It is a reminder that the darkness is comprehensive but the light is not overcome. Growing up, I lived out of the belief that love and acceptance were just out of reach and required enormous effort. My daughters will never think that, and I see how free they are because they don't.

▪ ▪ ▪

To be a Christian is to be crucified.

Yes, and: to be a Christian is to share in the resurrection. To be a Christian is to lay down your life and it is to receive God's Spirit and his kingdom. That's what my life was missing. I knew injustice and resistance, but I didn't know abundant life and beauty. I saw myself as a hammer in God's toolbox and a soldier in his army, not as his kid with a permanent seat at my Father's table. I threw myself into work, performing for acceptance, rather than being and receiving. I didn't see how light was breaking through every day in smiles, laughs, wonderful food, and good music from when I was younger through to today. I was too de-formed and deceived to notice.

So I allowed God to start re-forming me.

I needed an often-forgotten part of discipleship: God's clear and wonderful invitation to beauty and resistance in equal and ever-increasing measure, personally and corporately for our benefit and God's glory. This would also be the case if the opposite were true.

If my life had been saturated with beauty, and resistance were merely an afterthought, I would still need a healthy awareness of both. If I expected comfort instead of struggle, my daily life would inevitably be pierced by the suffering, distress, destruction, and upheaval of others—whether in my Instagram feed, through family members sharing links in the group chat, or during holiday conversations that would leave me anxious or concerned. Unhoused neighbors in need or peaceful protesters would disrupt my morning commute and I might want to make a change but feel unsure about where to begin.

Once I started to engage, issues like poverty, White supremacy, patriarchy, genocide, healthcare, and immigration would seem overwhelming. I'd tell myself that managing daily responsibilities was hard enough. So I'd likely end up turning up the volume on the headphones of my life, focus on more self-care, and try to filter out the sounds of war, mass shootings, and political turmoil—until it all became too loud to ignore again. Eventually, I'd feel that familiar sense of being overwhelmed, and the cycle of disruption, disengagement, outrage, and burnout would start all over.

God made us for more than this.

Wherever we find ourselves on the spectrum between resistance and beauty, whether through our history or preference, I am convinced a healthy life with Jesus holds an awareness of and engagement with both—usually at the same time. I am convinced we can build the scaffolding for a new life with Christ in pursuit of his beloved community together.

REST

2

why can't we rest?

There is no fear in love. But perfect love drives out fear.

1 JOHN 4:18

Miro is a beautifully designed digital workspace intended to help individuals and teams plan, brainstorm, organize, present, and even manage projects. It seemed like love at first sight. When I saw our project manager run a meeting using the tool, I thought, *This is going to be great.* So I started off pridefully on my own.

My board captured the thoughts in my head, the passions in my heart, and the work of my hands. In my mind it was all connected. And when I finally hit "share my screen," eyes got wide and I heard audible gasps from those not on mute. The breaths and stares were not of awe but confusion. This happened with my administrators, my wife, my supervisor, and a cohort I was leading. Not good.

I believe that's because when I started using Miro, I approached it like I do most matters of technology and organizing. I read half the instructions, skipped the templates, and watched the how-to videos at double speed. Our team's project manager used it brilliantly, so surely I could figure it out.

Clearly I had not. Where I saw light, wonder, and connection, others saw gaps, cracks, and disorder. I was trying to invite people to get to know me, and it was clear that I barely knew myself. I was not the rested, healthy person with a few growth edges I perceived myself to be. I was an overscheduled, overfunctioning leader whose inner life and intimacy with others did not mirror what I taught about. Of course I had grown, but instead of "arriving," I had a ways to go. And I was woefully unaware of it.

Perhaps you've been there. You think you eat or exercise a certain amount until you start to track your meals and activity. You think you don't curse that much until your loved ones make you put dollars in a swear jar. You think you spend a certain amount on coffee or eating out, but then you look at your budget or credit card bill. That was me—standing a little too close to the mirror again, and everyone could see it.

LIGHT FOR ME, GAPS FOR EVERYONE ELSE

I started using Miro to explain how organized I was, but what I presented was a mess. I wanted to live a life that prioritized loving God, myself, and my neighbors nearby and worldwide. What filled the connected laptops was not that.

Living this out had to begin in my heart and with the neighbors in my house—my wife and children. It had to display the priorities of someone with limits and boundaries while giving and receiving God's abundance with joy. That was missing completely.

The most difficult portions of marriage counseling sessions and personal prayer times echoed in my mind, and the basic tenets of faith rose to the surface. The Greatest Commandment had to move front and center.

> Love the Lord your God with all your heart and with all your soul and with all your mind and with all your strength. . . . Love your neighbor as yourself. (Mark 12:30-31)

I felt exposed. My integrity and well-being seemed at stake, so I doubled down on deflecting. I lacked inner resources, and I did not know how to create or leverage external support to live my call out in a way that flowed from my identity as a beloved child of God. I did not make plans or think things through. My work was reactive. As things came up and people asked questions, I responded. But I lacked a vision for the future. On top of that, I had not counted the cost of the house I was trying to build.

Those closest to me wanted to help. But I found myself making excuses or rejecting them outright, so my relationships lacked depth and reciprocity. I was too busy using all my energy projecting the self I hoped the world would see, approve of, and affirm.

I reflected the same patterns and narratives I had grown up with because I was not fully aware of them. After all, I cannot treat ailments I am unwilling to confess. By starting my Miro board, I unwittingly gave myself an opportunity to confess how lost I felt.

But I was too busy trying to appear competent.

If sabbatical was a peak, then there were valleys on both sides. Covid, two small kids, and my uninterrogated insecurities snuffed out the fire that burned so bright during that season. The good seeds that got planted were plucked up by the worries of the world, the deceitfulness of wealth, and my desires for other things.

I often felt powerless to fix my marriage and didn't have the energy for either my children or my extended family. Priscilla and I got into the same infinity loops, or negative communication patterns, about cleaning and my lack of care, concern, or willingness to learn.[1] I wouldn't confess my contributions to the problem and didn't want to discuss how it made me feel or my impact on her. I just wanted the fight to be over so I could move on to something that helped me not feel like a failure. To help me not to think, *I'm just like my dad.*

Looking back, I can see that I felt hurt frequently but couldn't admit it because I feared rejection. I had wants but rarely expressed them because I feared disappointment.

I had assumptions but feared that if I clarified them, the worst of what I believed about myself would be confirmed.

I couldn't rest because it was not an option. Accomplishment was how I defined myself and without it I felt lost. And lost was certainly what I was. The pandemic ended my work and my professional expectations. When I returned to work in the fall of 2020, no one could travel, and even when restrictions were lifted, they were firmly in place for me. We had two small children, and my mother-in-law with a chronic lung condition lived with us. Other people were trying to get back to normal, but isolation continued for our little pod.

So virtual programming and all the tools that came with it were my new normal. I moved to a different role in my organization, giving up all that was familiar. One thing stood out to me from the first meeting with my new team. I did not know who I was independent of the work I had done in the past. And that was on display for all to see on the digital tool that captured our collective efforts for eighteen months: Miro.

Instead of using the tool to show how organized and effective I was to everyone, I used Miro as a visual journal to pray, reflect, and be honest with myself.

Today, one section of my Miro board has black boxes with white writing, labeled for each month of the year from January to December. The month names are in bold font and underlined. I created these boxes in response to a prompt I received years ago, suggesting that I schedule things to look forward to. Although I made a note of this idea in a draft email to myself, I never took any action on it. The question is, why?

A clear reason is explained by the late professor, author, and theologian Dr. Robert Mulholland in his book *The Deeper Journey*. Mulholland said individuals who project a false self must build defenses to justify and protect that image. He writes:

> The reality of the "false self"—this pervasive, deeply entrenched, self-referenced structure of being as the primary context of our spiritual journey—is one of the hardest things for us to acknowledge. We tend to think of the false self as a "surface phenomenon" that can be treated by a few cosmetic alterations in our behavior. We are slow to accept the fact that our false self permeates all the way to the core of our being. It is hard to admit that we are profoundly habituated to a self-referenced way of being in the world that manifests itself in characteristics such as being fearful, protective, possessive, manipulative, destructive, self-promoting, indulgent, and making distinctions so as to separate ourselves from others.[2]

For example, if I wanted to appear wealthy, successful, and put together, my social media feed would reflect this image. I would post photos of my beautiful partner on vacation in exotic locations or dining at trendy restaurants. I might also share pictures of my latest purchases or seek advice on expensive gadgets, not because I need the advice, but to show that I'm considering these high-end items and project my elite status. In my own life, my marriage, friendships, and ministry became tools to maintain the façade I presented to the world. In a 2012 interview with activist and author Dana Roc, she asked if I saw my poetry and the ability to move people to action as a gift. My response was:

> When you see John Mayer pick up a guitar, you know that it would be a travesty if he didn't play the guitar. Like De La Vega, when he grabs paint cans, you're like "Dude was made to do graffiti in the park!" In the same way, if I didn't write, if I didn't speak, then I would be doing a disservice to the people around me because that's what I was actually put here to do. Not to glorify my own self, but to actually leave this world a better place than I found it. So, I would say it's a responsibility.[3]

When she asked about the legacy I wanted to leave in a hundred years, I responded with only a fraction of the Great Commandments. I told her, "If somebody looked at my life and thought, 'He really tried to love God with his heart, soul, and mind, and he loved his neighbor as himself,' if they thought that, then that would be cool."[4]

And that's true. It would be cool. But it wouldn't be totally Christlike. In the interview, I did nothing to articulate what a healthy love of self looked like in word or deed. Many alumni of my early ministry programs received the same toxic theological cocktail I did. When I implemented a retreat of silence in our weeklong spring-break discipleship programs and a weekly sabbath into my six-week summer leadership-development initiatives, one alumnus asked if he needed to intercede and intervene. He was implying that rest was wrong. I had discipled him and many others into wholesale adoption of my false self, and now he took it as doctrine.

This is an example of what Mulholland says is even more dangerous—a religious false self. He explains:

> For those on an intentional spiritual journey, our awareness of the deadly and debilitating nature of the religious false self is essential. Rigorous religious practices, devoted discipleship, sacrificial service, deeper devotional activities may do nothing more than turn a nominally religious false self into a fanatically religious false self. The essential difference between a false self and a religious false self is that the latter brings God into its life, but in service of its false self programs. Our religious false self may begin with a genuine experience with God. But then, like Peter on the mount of transfiguration, we often seek to contain our experience within a box of our own making. We attempt to integrate our experience with God into the

structures of our life in ways that are minimally disruptive to our status quo. The "God" within our box, however, becomes a construct, an idol, that enables us to maintain control of what we call "God" as well as continue to be in control of our existence.[5]

As an Enneagram Three, I crave significance and achievement and fear invisibility. Therefore, the people around me and the work I did were all in service to my being perceived as a good "Christian" man. I lived out of the lie that if people could see these things, I would finally be valuable; if people could see all of my good deeds, I would not be disposable.

Trying to gain my worth through activity and maintain my personal sense of value was a never-ending pursuit. I reflected the very same patterns and narratives I'd grown up with because I was not fully aware of them and certainly had not addressed them. If I explore that more deeply, I find that I am running away from my genogram.

A genogram is a creative way to display a family tree. It gives detailed data on relationships among family members and includes information about emotional and social relationships, medical history, and psychological dynamics. Various symbols are used to represent different individuals and relationships within a family. These symbols help provide a detailed and clear visual representation of family dynamics, relationships, and patterns over three generations.

In my genogram, the majority of marriages on both sides of my family suffered from estrangement and infidelity. I remember my mother encouraging me to look for men outside my family who could mentor me and I could emulate. Unconsciously, I concluded that if I didn't do what I saw in my family, I would be good enough. Instead of having a vision of masculinity and fatherhood informed by dreams, passions, and liberated visions of love, grace, and truth from Scripture and community, I succumbed to counter-formation.

In an effort to not be shaped by the brokenness in my genogram, I sought the opposite and in doing so was still shaped by it. That is counter-formation. I did not have a new vision—just another broken tree from a tainted seed. While reflecting on a difficult therapy session, I realized that I thought a good man was someone who didn't cheat on his spouse, had a job, and wasn't abusive or addicted to alcohol. This was the opposite of my genogram but a painfully low bar for my partner and my children.

My actions were not motivated by love; they were driven by fear. I worked hard because I feared being seen as lazy. I lived in constant fear of inappropriate relationships because I never wanted my children to experience the betrayal I felt as a child when witnessing infidelity in my family. And I was hyperconscious of how my behavior impacted my wife—so much so that my self-esteem and self-confidence were entangled with how I thought she was feeling toward me at all times. *Lord, have mercy.*

I was working so hard not to repeat the tank I grew up in that I was constructing a different type of terrarium. Life existed inside it, but the beings were still trapped. And I desperately wanted to be free. I did not know that rest—literally going to sleep—would be core to that process and how difficult that would be. I realize now that I was just not ready.

LEAVING MY FALSE SELF

Protecting my false self was my top priority, and I defended anything that supported that identity when it was threatened. I was determined not to repeat the patterns from my genogram, but I unconsciously recreated them. However, during my sabbatical, with new structures in place, I could take small steps toward building a different life. The simple prompt to create a new monthly calendar aligned with my conscious desires, and making practical changes moved from impossible to probable.

My wife used to complain that I consistently squeezed the margin out of our lives, and my children said I didn't spend enough time with them. This feedback left me feeling inferior and defective, and those feelings had become my reality. As I began my new journey, I asked myself where those feelings came from. With an understanding of my false self and my genogram, I could now make decisions that aligned with my deepest values rather than my deepest wounds and whims.

Instead of filling each month with work, events, and conferences, I needed to fill them with celebrations, holidays, birthdays, and new traditions. I had to exchange an audience of paying strangers for my family and being well-known by many for being significant to a few. This transition could be framed as a natural result of getting older or moving into a different life stage because of marriage and children. But something I have noticed and admired is that my students, friends, and confidants of various ages who celebrate well have deep connections with people around them and are able to hold love of neighbor, God, and self in tension to model Christ in beautifully resistant ways.

These efforts required two simultaneous actions to build a new life: remove rotten boards and replace them with new ones that embody beauty and resistance.

BACK TO THE MIRO BOARD

Looking at the year laid out in twelve perfect blank boxes in Miro, I had some decisions to make. For more than ten years, I had spent a week or two every May at a camp discipling college students and raising financial support for my ministry projects. Every summer I had spent eight weeks mentoring students who wanted to follow Jesus faithfully, integrating their professional lives with God's prioritization of justice and serving the least of these.

For most people, March through August is filled with opportunities for genuine connection and celebration, whether with family, a faith community, or friends. Mother's Day, Father's Day, my mother-in-law's birthday, and my younger daughter's birthday were wonderful chances to celebrate my family. Lent, Easter, and Pentecost were times I could have given and received deeply from my church. And Juneteenth, Memorial Day, and Independence Day were rich commemorative experiences that deserved my time, energy, and engagement.

However, I was often physically absent during these times. And when I was physically present, I was often emotionally and spiritually absent. Social media left me forever elsewhere, and the intensity of my experiences left me emotionally drained. I had the will to change but not the means. Two important moments showed me how I was pretending to be someone I wasn't and how that was hurting me and those I loved.

Cutting out date nights. In the summer of 2018, two interns worked with me on writing projects. They pored over drafts of my manuscript for *Twelve Lies That Hold America Captive* and early material for our Emotionally Healthy Activist Course.[6] As I was explaining the rule of life, I walked them through mine. While discussing restorative weekly rhythms, I realized that since their program had started, I took no sabbath and set aside no time with my wife. Date nights got cut for "Dinner and a Documentary," where my students and I would enjoy a meal and a film, then discuss how we felt and might act in response. Rest for myself and rest with my wife had been written out of the schedule to make space for the program these interns were participating in. I was not practicing what I was trying to preach, and it was all written down in my notebooks. The hypocrisy was deafening.

Ministry versus childbirth. This may have been a fresh discovery for me, but it was not new. In the summer of 2016, before my first daughter was born, I had a conversation with my wife about our birthing plan. We both knew that the six-week summer leadership-development program I directed was an intense time. And when she asked about meeting her at the hospital and interrupting the program, I resisted. I was more committed to ensuring the program's success than being present for my wife and newborn baby. Is ministry more important than the birth of my child?

This mindset was heavily influenced by listening to apologists such as Ravi Zacharias. Before his death, Zacharias was a prolific writer, speaker, and defender of the faith. I introduced him at two consecutive Veritas Forum events when I was a student at Columbia. One of the stories he told was about missing the birth of his daughter because he was preaching the gospel. I remember him saying with pride that his wife understood, and the crowd seemed to agree that he'd made the righteous choice. Looking back, I believe it was the wrong one—especially since Zacharias was eventually found to be an abuser.[7] He traveled extensively, blaming unfaithfulness to his wife, betrayal of his vows, and the exploitation of women and girls on the stress from his ministry.

I came to realize that not only was the genogram of my biological family important, but my spiritual lineage was as well. I had taken to heart the sermons of men who held destructive, misogynistic theologies—men like Mark Driscoll and John Piper, whose "Young, Restless, and Reformed" movement was prominent while I was in college.[8]

Both of these instances illustrate devotion to my false self and the fruit of my biological and spiritual genograms. They reveal how I could not bear being seen as unsuccessful, a failure, or anything other than a hard worker. On top of that, I wanted my wife to know how important that was to me and be invested in the same foolishness. I had a job and was respected by many people. Surely I was more than good enough? *Lord, have mercy.*

These two events cracked something in our marriage that is still in repair. Structure and support are required to maintain the integrity and relational trust I committed to. It is clear to me now that I had no scaffolding. I did not have the supportive, reflective habits in place that could help me align my values to my actions and live with consistency. And when they were available, I did not take them. I was in denial. Now I know I need rhythms of formation and repair to hold me up and together.

REMOVING ROTTEN BOARDS

If I was going to remove the boards that were rotting my marriage, stunting my relationships, and failing to hold me together, I needed scaffolding to keep me intact as I made changes. I needed support when things got difficult—because they would be difficult. My flesh is weak and the enemy is always prowling. As in the parable of the sower in Mark 4:19, I heard Jesus' word and the wisdom of others, but the worries of life, the deceitfulness of wealth, and the desire for other things choked the work and word of God. It became unfruitful. Individual and collective disciplines were necessary for the seeds God had planted to sprout and thrive.

During my sabbatical, my spiritual director Kimberly helped me ask questions about delight and press into the lies about my false self. My marriage counselor Kelly pushed me to address issues in my genogram, while Charles called me out in group and individual psychoanalysis. Finally, Carolyn invited me to reflect on how all I was learning and discovering might integrate into my work. During a time of reflection, God reminded me of a prayer time when someone saw an image of rotten railroad ties being removed and new tracks being put in. It was necessary, major surgery. God was doing a new thing, and it was time to join him.

WORKING OUT OF REST, NOT FOR IT

The fruit of this labor blossomed on the Miro board and has come to maturity over the past four years. My months of the year are no longer marked primarily by ministry and productivity but by rest and delight. I am not less productive or less busy. I am just not oriented around busyness and my false self. Table 1 shows what marks the twelve months for me now.

Table 1. Twelve months of beauty and resistance

January	February	March	April
• "DOPE DAY" • My birthday • MLK Day • Chinese New Year	• Valentine's Day • Annual snowboarding trip	• Lent • Everest's and mother-in-law's birthday (same day!)	• Easter • Spring break
May	**June**	**July**	**August**
• Mother's Day	• Father's Day • Juneteenth • Celebrate the end of the school year	• Vacation • Maia's birthday	• Baking bread on my mom's birthday to remember her
September	**October**	**November**	**December**
• Labor Day weekend • Hiking and apple picking	• Camping trip over Indigenous Peoples' Day weekend • More hiking!	• Hiking and seeing the foliage • Thanksgiving gathering in my hometown	• Priscilla's birthday • Enormous Christmas Eve party • New Year's Eve with close family and friends

DOPE Day

DOPE stands for Day of Planning Everything. My idea of a plan is to "figure it out," and Priscilla sits on the opposite side of that spectrum. So a DOPE Day gives us both something to look forward to and look back on. We mine the past year for themes of grief and celebration, lament and delight; and we record our goals for the coming year. Budgets, calendars, and how we will make decisions take

> shape during this eight-hour time of sharing delicious food
> and food for thought. This has been a grounding, at times
> stressful, but very fruitful time.

Today, I genuinely look forward to my times of rest, delight, and engagement with beauty as much as I do my times of work, service, and resistance. I also see how they overlap and intertwine to reflect the integrity I believe God made me for. I value sleep as much as productivity and I work to embrace my physical limits as much as my spiritual ones. I recognize that my family of origin and indeed my own will and personality pull me away from God and push me toward other things. I also recognize that there are larger social narratives at work, not just on me but on all of us, because research and stories from friends show that my struggle is not singular or unique.

When I started to share these reflections with friends, family, and colleagues, they resonated with them. Every person I knew was trying to navigate relationships with family and friends, to raise kids or try to have them and attain some sort of stability in a world reverberating with uncertainty. It seemed like we were living in a country and context that felt increasingly like it existed only for other people to thrive. Being a primary parent with a full-time job seemed to normalize this rat race, but God did not make me a rodent with a destiny to run forever.

One internal script I had to overcome was the idea that God was a master on a plantation. This lie was a false ideology holding others together. When I identified the dogmas and institutions reinforcing my unhealthy narratives, things became much clearer. I had to increase my level of emotional health, awareness, and maturity to engage the bigger picture well, and after I did that, I could assess what was in my control and what was not.

During my first few sessions with a spiritual director at the beginning of my sabbatical, I was struck by the revelation that God was not a master on a plantation but my heavenly Father who loved me deeply. This unlocked something deep within me, and I believe it could free something in all of us—it's a truth that must be named explicitly in our current context for Jesus followers to more fully reflect the freedom Christ afforded us through his life, death, and resurrection. After all, as Palestinian theologian Munther Isaac put it, "Theology without context is irrelevant."[9] So in the same way that the gospel must be good news to all people at all times, it also must be good news to all people in our specific season.

I believe that those of us living in a postcolonial era are in a season of deep intersectional crisis around race, class, gender, and the environment. This situation requires rigorous interrogation, deep discipleship, and embodied liberation. Historian Carter G. Woodson, author of *The Mis-education of the Negro,* said:

> If you can control a man's thinking you do not have to worry about his actions. When you determine what a man shall think you do not have to concern yourself

about what he will do. If you make a man feel that he
is inferior, you do not have to compel him to accept an
inferior status, for he will seek it himself. If you make a
man think that he is justly an outcast, you do not have
to order him to the back door. He will go without being
told; and if there is no back door, his very nature will
demand one.[10]

Woodson, the son of former slaves, understood that colonization is a complete process. And all of us live in the
wake of European expansion that is global in scope and
scale. Hierarchy, domination, incentives, and punishments
cover every facet of society like an intense, destructive, and
inescapable fog. European colonialism, which spawned the
Americas we know today, began with a corrupt ideology
that embedded itself within institutions to create, spread,
enforce, and defend its notions.

With colonial ideology widely adopted and enforced by
systems firmly in place, its proponents can scrutinize interpersonal interactions and establish protocols so that all people
under the dominant ideologies and institutions understand
their roles and responsibilities. At the same time, they demonstrate the consequences should the rules be violated.

Next, the settlers make known the laws and cultural expectations for the intimacies of life. These laws govern not
only how people are to interact in public but also how to
behave in private. This means the dominant culture and

its devotees decide who marries whom, how children are raised, who gets to do it, how sickness is treated, and more, until every area of life comes into alignment.

With all these things in place, the ideology is pressed all the way down to the individual level. When an ideology has been so effectively communicated and enforced throughout many generations, resistance feels futile at best and foolish at worst. Imagination is stifled, dissent is punished, and the dominant people and the power they hold remake people and society in the image they desire.

This is inherently opposed to God's good order because we are made in his image to flourish, work, steward, and create. Humankind was not created to make hierarchies of domination and use our power and resources to uplift ourselves, decide and protect what's "ours," and subjugate others in service to that violent purpose. We were made in the image of a loving, just, and wonderful God to reflect that awe and beauty in the world in harmony with him, one another, and all of creation.

In my context, White supremacy, patriarchy, and greed pressed me into a mold God did not make for me. I am made in his image to flourish, work, steward, and create. I was not formed in my mother's womb to have pale skin, perform dominant masculinity, or build my identity around what I could extract from myself, the environment, and everyone around me. That way of being requires ceaseless effort, unending defense, and constant expansion—and it is exhausting. Yet it manages to drive my individual and our collective dissatisfaction, despair, and desperation.

DISSATISFACTION

We feel dissatisfied as a population because we have been fashioned into consumers instead of stewards. Victor Lebow, an influential twentieth-century economist, said:

> Our enormously productive economy demands that we make consumption our way of life, that we convert the buying and use of goods into rituals, that we seek our spiritual satisfactions, our ego satisfactions, in consumption. The measure of social status, of social acceptance, of prestige, is now to be found in our consumptive patterns. . . . We need things consumed, burned up, worn out, replaced and discarded at an ever increasing pace.[11]

I'm not sure if Lebow was aware that one of the things burned up and worn out would be us. I was not meant to be a machine or measure myself and others by utility. But this truth is difficult to hold fast to. One reason for this hardship is advertising.

Advertisements sow seeds of comparison, lack, and discontent. In 2007, mass print and digital media bombarded us with five thousand ads per day.[12] Now with social media woven into the fabric of our lives and our phones inseparable from our hands, ads flow steadily toward us at nearly double that rate. Up to ten thousand ads reach a person in the United States each day during the five to six hours most of us spend on our phones.[13]

This dissatisfaction is tilled and sown, and the resulting fruit is that I need to change something. The solution to my dissatisfaction is extraction. Get more from my body with this workout. Get more from my partner with this technique. Or just get a new partner with this app. If I buy this product or visit this beach, I will finally have what I want. Pursuit as purpose is exhausting; it keeps us up at night, and the stress shortens our lives.[14] It exacerbates our risk of physical, emotional, and mental unhealth.[15] All of this because we seek contentment through effort and accumulation instead of learning to be content through Christ.

DESPAIR

This is the context of the oft-quoted Philippians 4:6-13:

> Rejoice in the Lord always. I will say it again: Rejoice! Let your gentleness be evident to all. The Lord is near. Do not be anxious about anything, but in every situation, by prayer and petition, with thanksgiving, present your requests to God. And the peace of God, which transcends all understanding, will guard your hearts and your minds in Christ Jesus.
>
> Finally, brothers and sisters, whatever is true, whatever is noble, whatever is right, whatever is pure, whatever is lovely, whatever is admirable—if anything is excellent or praiseworthy—think about such things.

Whatever you have learned or received or heard from me, or seen in me—put it into practice. And the God of peace will be with you.

I rejoiced greatly in the Lord that at last you renewed your concern for me. Indeed, you were concerned, but you had no opportunity to show it. I am not saying this because I am in need, for I have learned to be content whatever the circumstances. I know what it is to be in need, and I know what it is to have plenty. I have learned the secret of being content in any and every situation, whether well fed or hungry, whether living in plenty or in want. I can do all this through him who gives me strength. (Philippians 4:4-13)

Instead of making our requests known to God, we make them known to our bosses, parents, spouses, friends, strangers, children, delivery drivers, and the planet itself. And no matter how much we extract, we are not filled. King Solomon, who held himself back from no indulgence, exclaimed in Ecclesiastes 2 that it all was chasing after the wind. There is no contentment in amassing possessions, taking from others, or working day and night, says one of the wealthiest kings in human history. Yet I and many others think we will be the ones who reap different fruit from the same seeds.

This is the ideology of exceptionalism. We drank the Kool-Aid of the dominant class and are now distributors of this terrible drink, making persuasive invitations to run

instead of rest, to accumulate instead of abide. Go and
make a life for yourselves, says the dominant power of the
day, and we fall in line. What those in power fail to mention
is that this striving is exchanged for an abundant life with
God. We cannot serve two masters.

Trappist monk, writer, and theologian Thomas Merton
did not exclude those who seek justice in this context. Those
like me who are too focused on seeking justice for God can
mar our resistance if we don't leave the culture behind. In
his book *Conjectures of a Guilty Bystander,* Merton says:

> There is a pervasive form of contemporary violence
> to which the idealist most easily succumbs: activism
> and overwork. The rush and pressure of modern life
> are a form, perhaps the most common form, of its
> innate violence. To allow oneself to be carried away
> by a multitude of conflicting concerns, to surrender
> to too many demands, to commit oneself to too many
> projects, to want to help everyone in everything, is to
> succumb to violence. The frenzy of our activism neu-
> tralizes our work for peace. It destroys our own inner
> capacity for peace. It destroys the fruitfulness of our
> own work, because it kills the root of inner wisdom
> which makes work fruitful.[16]

Whether we are rolling with the culture or postured to
resist it, if Christ does not dwell within us, despair will set
in or we will permanently posture ourselves to keep it at

bay. Neither one of these realities is the shalom for which we were made.

Author and activist Tricia Hersey says in *Rest Is Resistance: A Manifesto* that "you were not just born to center your entire existence on work and labor. You were born to heal, to grow, to be of service to yourself and community, to practice, to experiment, to create, to have space, to dream, and to connect."[17] Relentless effort is plainly not what we were made for. It profoundly misshapes us, and as Merton and Hersey both say, it does violence to our souls.

Thus the burden of Whiteness and its supremacy is impossible to carry and maintain; it crushes us under its weight. Many scholars have highlighted the depths of despair in the United States population. Notably, among White Americans with a high school degree and lower, it is rising.[18] And instead of reentrenchment of a nativist, identitarian, or even skinhead neo-Nazi movements, there must be a powerful, consistent declaration that Galatians 3:26-28 is true:

> So in Christ Jesus you are all children of God through faith, for all of you who were baptized into Christ have clothed yourselves with Christ. There is neither Jew nor Gentile, neither slave nor free, nor is there male and female, for you are all one in Christ Jesus.

Please note that this is not a call for assimilation or uniformity, which defaults to Whiteness, patriarchy, greed, and domination, but a pursuit of Revelation 7, where the church on this side of heaven takes no pleasure in our segregation, stratification, or exploitation. Instead we mirror for our cities and towns what the disciples did in Corinth, Ephesus, Galatia, and Rome.

DESPERATION

If God's kingdom is not the goal, our own kingdom will become the aim. This is a plantation mentality in which there are masters, overseers, and the enslaved. Some are forced to work for little or nothing, while others are forced to supervise them to avoid a lower spot on the ladder of economic, racial, and gender mobility. Then there are those at the "top" seeking to maintain their dominance at all costs. We see this in corporations where there is no accountability for executives who steal millions of dollars or cause catastrophic accidents that kill and maim individuals and take the livelihoods of many more. CEO pay has increased by 1,460 percent since 1978.[19] In the same year, federal minimum wage was $2.65. It was increased to $7.25 in 2009 and has remained unchanged.[20]

There is nothing restful about lives lived under this ideology, within institutions where violence and greed are markers of efficiency and effectiveness. I know this not only because my genogram, life, and relationships have exemplified this stressful, weary way of being but also because the fruits of our society testify to this fact.

Dr. Bernice Johnson Reagon was a field secretary for the Student Nonviolent Coordinating Committee (SNCC), founding member of the Freedom Singers, and a participant in the female acapella group Sweet Honey in the Rock. She was a holder of Black wisdom, beauty, and resistance through song. She committed Matthew 11:28-30 to song, and it is a Spirit-filled invitation to get off the hamster wheel, treadmill, and conveyor belt of false identity and struggle for a sense of sovereignty that simply never comes.[21] Jesus says in Scripture:

> Come to me, all you who are weary and burdened, and I will give you rest. Take my yoke upon you and learn from me, for I am gentle and humble in heart, and you will find rest for your souls. For my yoke is easy and my burden is light. (Matthew 11:28-30)

I do not believe it was a coincidence that Jesus invited us into rest. As Solomon said, there is nothing new under the sun, so it is my fervent prayer that we as his body would say yes.

WE NEED DELIVERANCE AND DISCIPLESHIP

Core to following Jesus is deliverance and discipleship. Often faith communities in our current context prefer one or the other, and this is detrimental to individual walks with God and our collective witness to the world.

Deliverance without discipleship sanctifies the worst parts of the human experience. Discipleship without deliverance produces a self-referencing spirituality independent of a relationship with God. Both the instantaneous spiritual work of God and our deliberate choices are essential to a deep, formative life with Christ that produces fruit in us and in the world. We are delivered from demons, death, sin, hell, and the grave, and through discipleship we walk in victory out of brokenness toward personal and collective healing.

The tension between a being a person of productivity and usefulness as opposed to being rooted in inherent worth, dignity, and value was modeled for me from the time I entered the strawberry fields with my family at nine years old, was tracked academically into a different classroom at five years old, and saw our furniture repossessed in the fourth grade. I listened to conversations on the farm, overheard conversations between adults in the living room when I was supposed to be sleeping, and soaked up positive reinforcement in classrooms tied to my effort. All this groomed me for a life of work and productivity—not as the fruit of an abundant life with God but as a way to attain and communicate my own worth and value. And consequently I used the same measure to judge the value of others.

The same is true for many of us who claim to follow Jesus but live uninterrogated lives where our faith is entangled with hierarchies around race, gender, class, and the environment and our families and experiences dictate how we follow Jesus more than our Savior's example.

I remember sitting with a friend who was in a relationship where his financial needs were taken care of. For the first time in his life, he had a partner who communicated clearly that he could take whatever job he desired. Suddenly the pressure to perform and provide was released, and now he was stuck. What did he truly want to do?

Another friend spoke openly with me about the internal monologue that was on repeat after an unexpected layoff. Was a single, middle-aged man without a job worth anything? In a burst of honesty he blurted out, "I cannot be seen as another lazy Black man."

I sat across from a woman in ministry whose commitments stretched across all seven days in the week along with her full-time job as a nurse. How could she leave the students, mentees, and patients who needed her so urgently to rest? After we talked about the sabbath, she looked up and said, "There is just no time for that." All three of these people believed something deep that kept them from accepting Jesus' invitation to abide in him and have life.

Jesus and his kingdom offer us a new and better way of being this side of heaven. He is our cornerstone for a life and identity rooted in rest in Christ instead of an identity that waxes and wanes with our income, status, physical ability, appearance, or perceived usefulness to God and others. Beauty and resistance begin with willingness to lay down each day in him and rise each day with him, knowing full well that he alone is sovereign, knows all, and is everywhere at once. And we don't have to be.

RESTORE

why aren't we restored?

After I had experienced true rest, I could receive the truth that I was valuable independent of my effort and performance. But without cultivating healthy habits and relationships, I could easily slip back into former patterns. Through spiritual direction and difficult conversations I was better able to discern what people, patterns, and practices filled my mental, emotional, physical, and spiritual cups. I stopped running on adrenaline, chasing dopamine and "likes" online or words of affirmation in real life.

I identified the people I wanted to see each week, podcasts to listen to each day, my favorite workouts, and baking for genuine pleasure. Earl Grey macarons, homemade pizza, and Peloton meditations gave me things to look forward to that had nothing to do with achievement or accomplishment.[1] I could resist the internal voice that said I needed to be busy and the destructive lie that I was lazy. I could pause and enjoy the beauty God made available, and that was good. This was replenishment. This was what restoration looked, felt, sounded, and tasted like. Determining these things and layering them over my life held me together when I felt exposed and vulnerable. These rhythms were forming me into a freer person. Free to be more present to myself, others, and God. Free to give and receive love.

Homemade Pizza Recipe

Homemade pizza on Friday night was essential for slowing me down throughout the day and preparing for sabbath because the dough had to rise and be ready for our time together that night. Here's my recipe:

Ingredients: one pack active dry yeast, one cup warm water, three cups AP/00 flour, two tablespoons sugar, a half teaspoon salt, and two tablespoons olive oil.

Dissolve the yeast in the warm water with the sugar and let it rest for five minutes. Make sure the water is not hotter than 115 degrees, otherwise you'll kill the yeast and your dough won't rise. Add the salt to your flour. Make a well in the middle of the flour and pour the warm water in. Knead the dough until it is smooth and elastic and bring it together. Then add your oil and form the dough into a ball. Grease a medium bowl and put your dough in it. Cover with a damp towel and allow to rise in a warm, draft-free place for thirty minutes or until it doubles in size. Preheat the oven to 425 degrees. Grease one fourteen-inch pizza pan or two ten-inch pizza pans with an oil of your choice. Then stretch the pizza crust to fit the pan. Top and spice as desired.

Tip! I prebake my crust for about ten minutes to keep the cheese from browning—unless you like that!

I came to recognize I am an exponentially more kind, patient, and attentive person after I have had a good night's sleep. With every thirty minutes of uninterrupted shut-eye, I become a better listener and more attuned to the thoughts and feelings of those around me. I care about what my wife and children say and seek to understand them as they are rather than through the filter of my assumptions or annoyances. I know this because of what happens every day around 7:30 p.m.

Somewhere deep in my subconscious I am convinced that at this time, my children should be washed, dressed, teeth brushed, prayed for, and blessed to sleep. I have told myself that "Baba" is off the clock and my children become problems to be solved, not tiny humans to be loved. Instead of loving, I am irritable and short. These are just some of the signals that my rhythms of restoration are not enough.

I wish this lack of kindness and gentleness was confined to my home and those few hours each day, but that's not true. In the middle of the day, even after solid hours of rest overnight, I can be prideful, unkind, and dismissive. The suffering of others becomes an inconvenience for me as I feel stressed or stretched. Overwhelmed, I lose my ability to live out of my deepest values and choose comfort, convenience, and survival instead. I preach that I want to love my neighbor, but in practice, my actions don't match those words.

This is a common occurrence on our commute home: a woman in need approaches our car. She is at the stoplight selling mangoes as her daughter hangs on her back.

She becomes a distraction I want to avoid. I shove her and her humanity away. She becomes a cone to be avoided in the desired trajectory of my day, not a daughter made in the image of God making ends meet on the edges of our economy. I beat myself up for not having cash, setting a bad example for my kids, and being a bad Christian.

On other days, I decide whether to answer the people texting or calling my phone based on whether they are going to complicate or complement my day. In the end I usually send them to voicemail or leave as unread with no intention of going back because I just don't want to be bothered. Then I feel guilty for not making the time to check in and reach out. In both cases, I resort to living in reaction instead of with intention and within limits. This type of existence doesn't just have negative interpersonal impacts; it has systemic effects as well.

When I spend my money as a consumer in pursuit of comfort, convenience, and survival instead of as a steward of what God has given me to invest as best I can in the flourishing of my neighbors, the effects ripple far. Plastic utensils and other single-use plastics litter my car and backpack, because I might be well rested but I am overcommitted and not well planned. This contributes to the nearly ten billion tons of convenience-driven waste in landfills, waterways, oceans, and soil today.[2]

Likewise, I waste food because I don't organize the fridge, and that spoiled nourishment fills the local landfill because

I haven't figured out how to compost properly and keep pests away. That leads to more money spent that could have been allocated toward savings or generosity.

These and other examples of the dis-integration of my actions and values litter my life. If I haven't showered or eaten a solid meal, am dehydrated after back-to-back meetings, or encounter a real emergency, order flees. I lack the skills and structures to give myself good boundaries and the will and means to keep them. The changes I desire within myself and want to reflect in the world are not scaffolded, so I fall apart. And when I share my predicament with others, I find that they are falling apart too.

Some might be rested, but most are lonely and running the race of life in pursuit of comfort, stability, and security for themselves and their families through blunt effort. Like me, they have moments of clarity when the seeds of the gospel land and inspire temporary changes. However, the individual and communal habits and practices that encourage us during hard times and lovingly confront us when we get off track are often lacking or nonexistent.

WHAT I ACTUALLY NEED

What I actually need is not just rest each night but daily rhythms of restoration. My body, mind, and spirit require regular nourishment to stay grounded in the abundance of the Lord each day. Without these markers to orient myself toward beauty and resistance, I turn inward. Pride, narcissism, and hurry define how I engage with people and situations around me. I allow greed, anxiety, and the need to feel significant and valuable—ideas and institutions contrary to the kingdom of God and the good news of Jesus—to determine my self-perception as well as my posture and behavior toward others. A dangerous cycle continues where I am unable to perceive what is impacting me and cannot see how my thoughts, words, and actions impact others. Instead of having an abundant life and thriving in loving shalom, I exist in constant striving to project and protect my false self.

For a season at my church, one of the guys was a relentless recruiter. Phil gathered forty men in a group chat and got weekend warriors, park legends, and young bucks out for weekly pickup basketball games. It became a staple in my life and the lives of those who gathered. It was there I realized I was certainly not going to the NBA, connecting with others was more important than winning the game, and my jumper would never be better than my defense. This rhythm was made possible for forty of us because one guy invited us into his life.

BUILDING A DIFFERENT HOUSE

If rest is the foundation, the rhythms of restoration are the walls, studs, and joists. When we are well rested, we are better able to discern what people, patterns, and practices fill our mental, emotional, physical, and spiritual cups, and we are able to pour out and participate in the mutuality God made us for. These are necessary for a house to stand.

This affects not just my capacity to stand individually but allows my community to thrive collectively. My flourishing is inextricably linked with that of my neighbor and creation because my abundance, in the kingdom of God, is not meant to be a product of their poverty.

During my sabbatical in 2019, I realized my life was consumed by a need to prove my value. Why? The televised destruction of Black bodies, paired with Trump's ascendancy, formed within me a feeling of deep worthlessness and a belief that I was disposable. It was only through therapy, spiritual direction, and intentional times with God in community and solitude, rest, and action that I was able to reorient my life and resist the temptation to strive for acceptance and value already conferred on me by God. An abundant life can be had through deep, loving, and truthful engagement with ourselves, God, neighbors, and the environment.

To receive this, I was asked basic questions that I had to work hard to answer.

HOW DO I DELIGHT?

"How do you delight?"

This is the question my spiritual director Kimberly asked me when we first started meeting during my sabbatical. I was confused by her question. *I don't* is what I thought, but I'm sure some Sunday school answer slipped out, and she and I both knew it was nonsense. I may have mentioned writing and poetry to fend off the silence, but I don't actually remember. I do remember her head tilting slightly and the thought occurred to me that I couldn't fool her. I was stumped and embarrassed. What in my life would not bring me attention or accolades professionally, didn't provide any sort of income or sense of productivity, and could bring me joy?

The answer turned out to be baking. And now one of the core rituals of my life is all things gluten and delicious. (Don't worry, I can make gluten-free deliciousness too!) During Christmas when I was a child, my mother would bake pans of yeast rolls and deliver them as gifts to our family up the road. I grew up in a family with three siblings, and we shared 225 acres of land with five aunts and uncles and many cousins. My mother baked a lot of bread. Moreover, every August when one of my aunts visited from Philadelphia, we waited by a warm oven and made phone calls to let people know one pan was coming out and another one was going in. That meant hot bread was being buttered and if you didn't get a piece, another would be ready in twenty minutes.

On my birthday, Momma would bake me a pound cake, and as it came out of the oven, she, my younger brother, and I would wait until it was barely cool enough. Then we would eat the entire thing. There was nothing like the crunch of that Bundt cake's crust in contrast with that moist crumb. Bread was a redemptive piece of my genogram, so it made sense that when I slowed down, it made its way back into my life.

I shared this with Kimberly, and she gave me an assignment that felt more like an experiment. Kimberly told me to bake a pound cake. I was to be on the lookout for an opportunity, like my momma did, to make something for someone to show that I cared about them while also doing something that brought me joy. So I made a vanilla pound cake for a friend who lost his aunt.

I prayed for him while I mixed wet and dry ingredients together and didn't listen to an audiobook or a podcast. Instead I reflected on what it's like to lose someone and asked God to come near him, like he had done for me when my momma died. After the cake was done, I got on the subway and met him on his lunch break at a construction site. We ate in his truck and shared memories of his aunt, and three-quarters of that loaf disappeared. I did not get paid and it wasn't in a fancy box, just aluminum foil. It was difficult and delightful to be present with my friend in his grief. I did not end his suffering but was able to be present with him through it. Like the song "Afio Mai" says, "He never told us that it would be easy but he promised peace."[3] Jesus gave us that and I was grateful.

Pound Cake Recipe

Preheat your oven to 350 degrees and grease a nine-by-five loaf pan with coconut oil or butter, or use parchment paper for an easy lift-out. If you're doing this, make sure to cut a piece of parchment paper that hangs over the side. My momma used a Bundt pan! So that's my preference. This recipe is vegan but it doesn't have to be. Make it however brings you joy and suits your stomach.

Ingredients: A half-cup of vegan butter, a cup of white sugar, a teaspoon of vanilla extract, two teaspoons of lemon extract, a cup of vegan buttermilk (almond or soy milk mixed with a tablespoon of fresh lemon juice), two cups of all-purpose flour, three teaspoons of baking powder, a half teaspoon of salt, and two tablespoons of lemon zest.

Cream butter and sugar together and then add the vanilla and lemon extract. Make the buttermilk on the side and wait a couple minutes for it to curdle. Little bits should appear. Add that to your creamed sugar and butter in a standing mixer or grab that wooden spoon and mix it in.

In a separate bowl sift flour, baking powder, and salt together. Mix the wet and dry ingredients together and *don't overmix*. Put in the lemon zest and then pour the thick batter into the pan. Bake it for an hour. If you don't like it being super brown on top, at forty minutes tent some aluminum foil on top of it and put it back in the oven. Use a skewer or chopstick to make sure it's baked all the way through.

Now, this next step is optional but delicious. I cover my pound cake in sugar syrup. Take a half-cup of sugar and a half-cup of water and boil it on the stove. Whisk as this is happening and then take it off the heat after sugar is dissolved. Take some lemon juice and squeeze it into the mixture for an extra-punchy flavor. *After* it has cooled, take a pastry brush and paint to your heart's content.

After all that, eat the whole thing in one sitting with some good friends! And before you ask, of course you can store it for later. Delight in as much or little as you like.

BAKING BEAUTY AND RESISTANCE

When I bake, I don't have to go slow, but I can never be in a hurry. And whatever it is—fudgy brownies, yeast rolls, four-layer lemon cake, bacon-cheddar-scallion biscuits—I have to make a plan. I have to be deliberate and intentional, and I practice it to get better. I am never paid. My momma baked out of necessity to feed us, and now it feeds my soul, family, and friends. My enslaved ancestors baked by force, and now I can by choice. Every time I break bread I remember my neighbors with no food, those who don't have community like I do, and those who made my food possible.

I cook and give thanks, grieved and grateful. I hold the beauty and resistance at the same time in both hands, fully present to both and nourished—not depleted—by fully engaging with them at the same time. Alone or with my girls I pray, "Jesus, thank you for this food. Bless it to our bodies and our bodies to your service. Be with those who don't have food today and those who made this meal possible. May they experience the same freedom, fellowship, and provision you've given us so generously. Amen."

I wish I didn't have to learn to do this. The work is internal, external, individual, communal, and uphill, and I am doing it. These prayers and practices hold me up and hold me together amid the shifts. I am deeply grateful for those who taught and are still teaching me.

Bacon-Cheddar-Scallion Biscuits

Preheat oven to 425°F.

In a medium-sized bowl, put one tablespoon each of salt, garlic powder, and baking powder, a half teaspoon of baking soda, two cups of organic all-purpose flour, one cup of almond milk (vegan) with a tablespoon of lemon juice added OR one cup of buttermilk or milk, and four tablespoons of butter, vegan butter, coconut oil, or bacon fat—all of them are delicious. Be generous with the butter or other fat that you choose. Add two tablespoons minced garlic, a half cup of finely chopped scallions, a half cup of shredded cheddar cheese, and a half cup of crispy, fried bacon. Note: When you fry the bacon, save some of the fat and use it to grease one or two baking sheets. This will give texture and taste to your biscuits.

Mix all the ingredients together until the dough is sticky and smooth. It will not be a uniform ball or pretty to look at but should smell like delicious potential. Be careful not to overmix. You don't have to mash out chunks of butter or make sure the scallions are evenly distributed. Just mix with a wooden spoon or spatula until the flour is fully incorporated. After that, take a serving spoon and scoop out dollops of dough evenly across your bacon-greased pan. It fine to put the biscuits about two to three inches apart because they will not spread much.

Bake for eleven minutes and enjoy. Pray for those who made your meal possible and those who desperately need one just like it.

AN INTERVENTION

When Priscilla and I had our oldest daughter, it was easy for me to affirm her ethnic identity and cultural heritage—at least her mom's side. I looked into her eyes early on and affirmed that she was Chinese and Korean. But I didn't know how to explain being Black to her without dropping the comprehensive knowledge of terrible oppression and violence on her at the same time. White supremacy, anti-Blackness, and the mix of the two in misogynoir formed a yoke I did not want to give her.[4] I thought the history of enslavement, segregation, and enduring subjugation would break her neck. I believed it had broken mine, and I was not a woman of color in this violent, racist, patriarchal world.

Still, her three-year-old mind wondered, and she asked, "Mama is from China and Korea. Baba, where are you from?"

My ancestors whispered from the depths of the Atlantic Ocean in a language I don't understand, so I uttered, "Virginia." This place—not where Whiteness and Blackness were created, but where they took shape—innovated and scraped humanity out of humans like a spoon scraping meat out of a coconut because it was time for it to be consumed.

"Baba, Mama speaks Chinese. What do you speak?"

Instinctually, I sucked my teeth as if my genes were angered by her question. "English," I said. I was reminded that I needed to explain freedom and liberation to her in terms determined by the people who took it from us in the first place. I didn't need 23andMe; I needed branches on my family tree not to be anonymous. All of this was too much, so I avoided it for the first few years of her life entirely.

I did not know how to model healthy handling of the wonders and wounds of my family's history—the pain and the joy, the oppression and the freedom, the beauty and the resistance of our people. But I was challenged by my siblings on a Zoom call to tell my daughter she was Black. And that it wasn't oppressive racial constructs that defined us by chains and whips. I could allow our ancestors who clapped, sang, prayed, and swayed their way through each day, week, month, and year to tell her who we were—to tell me who I was. Rhythm was in her bones because it was in her Daddy's grandmommas on both sides. Black and Cherokee from south central Virginia—Brodnax and Keysville in Mecklenburg and Prince Edward. But for me to tell her, I had to hear it myself. I had to learn to dance like I didn't care, pray like I needed God to make it each day, and cook food that smelled so good that people forgot to pray. I had to be secure in who I was, whose I was, and my place in the kingdom and on earth.

SONG AND DANCE

Country music woke me up on Saturday mornings and gospel got me out of bed on Sundays. Momma would sway as she swept the floor and rock back and forth in the fourth pew from the front in our little wooden church. Motown emanated from our basement and hip-hop and R&B got recorded on blank cassettes in my bedroom. We danced to all of it. Music and movement were the tendons that connected the households on our road and in our community.

Scholar, singer, and activist Bernice Johnson Reagon said every Black person is walking around with 150 songs on our hearts. She founded Sweet Honey in the Rock, sang before Rev. Dr. Martin Luther King Jr., and took the stage for his "I Have a Dream" speech. And I can tell you she was right.

When my mother was going home to be with Jesus in September 2015, my brothers and I sang song after song in her room. There were no books, hymnals, or Googling of lyrics. Just the songs on our hearts that were handed down to us. We needed this rhythm and ritual from down deep.

Further back in my own life, verses came out when I was a teenager consumed by anger. Momma saw me seething and exasperated. She told me to "do something constructive or go punch a tree." I punched a white oak in the front yard. Then I grabbed a pen and wrote:

Poetry is my release
My shield from all grief
My refuge to which I retreat
When this world is too much for me
These phrases on these pages
The language my mind speaks
Metaphors and similes
Poetic elements I just breathe. . . .

This was a different yoke—a yoke, yes, but one that was easy and light. Not because it didn't have weight but because when I carried it, I felt free and purposeful. Jesus said in Matthew 11:28-30, "Come to me, all you who are weary and burdened, and I will give you rest. Take my yoke upon you and learn from me, for I am gentle and humble in heart, and you will find rest for your souls. For my yoke is easy and my burden is light."

I was weary and I came, and he gave me rest and restoration in him. This liberative yoke fastened me to my peace—Jesus. I was held together by Jesus and up by the sincere, loving invitations of my wife and siblings. That is what I needed to give to Maia.

A POEM FOR ME, A POEM FOR MAIA

So I wrote a poem for my eldest. Words to hold her up and keep her together the way they scaffolded me. Most days, since she was three years old, Maia has spoken these words:

Black is beautiful
Chinese is too
Korean is marvelous
All of this is true
Indigenous people bear the image of God
I am Cherokee on Matinecock land
My elders are from far and wide
And I know who I am
My color curve and curl is good
No matter what they say
My eye shape is God-ordained
I pray this every day

That I and all will know
That God makes no mistakes
God is not ashamed of me
So I am unashamed
The Father is before me
So I am unafraid
The Son is beside me
So I am unafraid
The Spirit is within me
So I am unafraid
My family is behind me
So I am unafraid
In Jesus' name
Amen

I gave my daughter what I had, and by God's grace it laid a foundation of beauty and resistance for both of us. Three years later, it was time to build some walls. One morning when she was six years old, Maia was getting ready for Culture Day at school, when students and teachers wore outfits representing their heritage. The year before, Maia had worn a qípáo (旗袍), and since our good friends had gotten her a dress from Ghana, I suggested she wear it that day. With confusion, she looked at me and said, "But I'm not from there." This was the moment.

Here is where I could try to connect with her and connect the dots between what I knew and how I knew it. I chose connection and curiosity and tried to clear up the confusion, but I had to remember I was trained to work with college students. My daughter was six years old and wanted to know why she should wear a Ghanaian dress. Fortunately, the seed we had planted had been nurtured, and it was about to bear fruit.

The poem she had been saying for three years prepared both of us for this moment. It was time to connect her braids and skin tone to something that at thirty-six years old I still had a hard time articulating outside of poetry. Now I needed to put it into prose.

So I finished tying up her hair and said, "Well, Maia, if they ask you today what your culture is, you can do a poem for them."

Confused, she asked, "What poem is that?"

I looked at her and said, "Black is beautiful," and held up one finger.

"Chinese is too," and I held up another.

"Korean is marvelous," and I raised one more.

She chimed in, "All of this is true."

Then we said together, "Indigenous people bear the image of God; I am Cherokee on Matinecock land. My elders are from far and wide, and I know who I am."

With four little fingers raised and a big smile on her face, she realized the poem told the story of her heritage, and though she didn't feel comfortable in the dress, she did feel confident in her skin, hair, eyes, and style. And that is more than I could ask or hope for at this age and stage in her life. Our daily practices held us together so that when the pressure of this moment came, we stood on our values and beliefs and were not crushed by the social yoke placed upon us. We were scaffolded and now my second daughter, Everest, is too.

My daughters know so much joy, abundance, and love. And I am deeply grateful for all that we have. Baking for them at first and now with them grounds us when things are chaotic, is beautiful when things are hard, and is simple when joy feels complicated. Praying for them and now having them pray for me is something holy and good, but those two words don't communicate the magnitude of the goodness I see, feel, and experience in those moments.

It is these regular, incredible encounters with goodness that intertwine resistance to injustice with the reception and pursuit of beauty in every portion of our lives. I believe this is especially true when an individual or community is on the bottom side of an oppressive power structure. Beauty can be fleeting, and moments of respite are rare, so restoration feels constantly out of reach. However, with community and intentionality, I believe we can find replenishment and the joy of the Lord.

My family's Friday nights are modeled after the Pizza Fridays we experienced with the Gaboury family. Jason and Sophia Gaboury were longtime campus ministers in New York City. When they were home on Fridays, there was a standing invitation for folks to come, sit, and eat. But because people do not live by bread alone, there was nourishment there that was more filling than slices of pizza.

When Priscilla and I made our way to their apartment over a decade ago, I saw in their living room what it looked like to pray with daughters. I saw liturgy modeled in a way that was accessible, not oppressive. I had no idea what Advent was other than the books that popped up for sale in my social media feeds before Christmas. But with the Gabourys, I saw how rhythms of prayer and reflection on Scripture held their family up and together and continues to do so. I know they were not perfect parents because they told me so. But I know their children love them. And because they had family disciplines that included encouragement, reflection, and blessing, not a rod or a backhand, that love has only grown between them.

My wife and I cried reflecting on what we saw that day. It was beautiful because these two girls were experiencing abundant love, grace, and truth from the two people they needed the most in the world. It was a picture of resistance because Jason and Sophia refused to allow the patterns that had violated the purposes of God in their own lives to be passed on to their children. Their daughters got the best of what each of them had to offer each day.

Looking back, I realize I had no idea how difficult it would be to incorporate liberative disciplines into our own lives. But I know viscerally how opposed powers and principalities are to that reality.

THE PRINCIPALITIES NEVER REST

The first time I ever went on vacation was my honeymoon. I was twenty-five and had never traveled somewhere that wasn't for work or school with my own money. My wife changed that, and every year since then, we have gone on vacation for two weeks. At first I fought the rhythm, like a dance with a beat my chest didn't recognize. Now I look forward to those nine days in an RV in Zion National Park or late nights with desserts and board games in Virginia. I now realize I didn't want to look forward to things like this because I feared disappointment. Without support from people who loved me and the personal skills and awareness to overcome setbacks, I told myself the story that vacation "wasn't worth it." My head knew that was not true, but my heart held fast to it because of situations like this.

While on vacation in the summer of 2022, our family went on a zipline course with a group of other tourists on Catalina Island off the coast of Southern California. The landscape was epic and streaking through air above the trees was exhilarating. But a familiar feeling interrupted my joy—the anxiety of exclusion. I was the only Black person in the group. I committed myself to trying to enjoy the moment, because the tickets were not cheap. Then our White tour guide started asking questions.

On the platform at the top of each new line she threw out an icebreaker to the group. Her first question to me was, "What's your greatest fear?" My internal response was, *One of my neighbors calling the police because there is a Black man at my house, and my daughters losing their dad in the driveway to police who shoot within seconds of arrival.* But of course I could not say that in front of all these White people. My momma raised me to prioritize White comfort, because that meant I would always make it back home. So what came out of my mouth was, "This. I am jumping off a perfectly safe platform even though I have children to live for." Everyone laughed. Deflection successful.

At the next platform, the guide asked, "What would be your last meal?" My internal answer: Fried chicken, biscuits, mashed potatoes, watermelon, and every other stereotypically Black and objectively delicious dish that my people so generously prepare for one another and had to prepare for y'all by force. My external answer: "Whatever the wonderful ladies at the church I grew up at are willing to serve me." Everyone laughed again. Another deflection successful. That pattern continued. And as I skimmed the tops of trees on the last leg, I was glad the tour was ending.

I had gotten used to jumping off the platforms. But I'll never get used to jumping out of my skin. Afterward, the members of the tour group went back to our segregated and stratified communities. Later that week, in a suburb of Los Angeles, I was cleaning my mother-in-law's car when a White woman crossed the street directly toward me. She was focused and intent. But at the last moment, when she was within feet of the car, she turned onto the sidewalk and walked in a different direction, headphones in, not paying attention to me at all.

So why did I experience her like a Russian fighter jet buzzing an F-15 off the coast of Alaska?[5] Why did my watch pick up an increased heart rate? Because I was in a town where White supremacists had rallied not too long before, and no one seemed aware that the blue-striped flags on the surrounding houses made me feel unwelcome.[6] The woman walked out of sight. But my adrenaline kept me wondering if I was doing anything White people might find suspicious. I looked down at my glass bottle of ginger beer. Could she have suspected that I was drinking in public? Would I be executed and become a hashtag for having an open container? Anti-Blackness and White supremacy are real and still reign, and they left me weary after those ten days.

NOWHERE FEELS LIKE HOME

On our way back home to Queens, I was glad to be going to a place where there were safe friends who believed I belonged. I lay down in a bed where I could sleep in peace, knowing my skin wasn't an anomaly and I had a community where I didn't have to deflect or code-switch.[7]

But then one morning not long after we got home, I was doing yard work in a hoodie. A White resident of our neighborhood stopped her car while driving by. She rolled her window down to tell me with a chuckle, "You better not have that hood on. People are gonna start asking questions." This was not the last time she did this. The next time she added, "I thought I needed to call the police." Both times I looked at her, smiled, and said as nonthreateningly as I could, "You're right about that." Both times she laughed and drove away.

I spent the next minute removing her from the list of White people who were safe for me and my kids. I spent the next ten minutes trying to figure out how to tell my wife what had happened. I spent the next hour trying to remind myself why we'd moved to this neighborhood. And I spent the day trying to plan how I would act when I saw her next. All this mental and emotional energy just to deal with the intractable reality that Whiteness doesn't take a vacation when I do—it's waiting for me where I'm headed and when I get home.

And it's not just White supremacy and anti-Blackness that are unrelenting. First Peter 5:8-9 describes the devil as a roaring lion seeking someone to devour, and in Ephesians 6:12 Paul talks about our battle being against powers and principalities. The destructive principality of patriarchy at work in my own heart is an idea that doesn't need sleep or rest. Similarly the institutions that hold oppressive ideologies in place are forever at work and ever adaptive.

I must replace and repair my heart, habits, and practices so I don't perpetrate or perpetuate those patterns against my own wife and children. Jesus warned everyone against being deceived by wealth, teaching that we cannot serve two masters. However, in a society that measures well-being by the ability to produce, consume, and accumulate, the temptation for more, better, and faster is relentless.

Therefore, to truly flourish in this life, I need not only deliverance from the power of death, sin, hell, and the grave but discipleship into individual and collective rhythms of encountering the living God and the kingdom he promises. I also need to observe and receive the beauty of it and participate in resistance to systems and structures that oppose it.

Jesus came to make all things new, so his freedom, love, and justice are as fierce and comprehensive as the injustice, violence, and discord that mark so much of my life and the world around me. My restoration must not depend on a society that wasn't designed for it. If I don't establish rhythms of replenishment, adapt when they are disrupted, and stay flexible as challenges arise, I will burn out in my pursuit of beauty and resistance.

Moreover, though I am made in the image of God, if I fail to build scaffolding for my own healthy formation and resist a loving community calling for faithful growth, I risk projecting my own image through control and domination. Left to my own will, I attempt to reshape the world in my likeness and yield to a vision determined by the patterns of the world (Romans 12:2) and the prince of the power of the air (Ephesians 2:2), not the Prince of Peace and the kingdom of heaven. I believe the same is true for all of us. Our tendency toward pride, narcissism, hurry, and self-worship are the reasons we cannot be fully restored, and they are precisely what we must resist when we choose to orient ourselves toward beauty and resistance.

This is true for anyone seeking to thrive as a human being and not just a producer and consumer of goods and services. I have seen my wife, Priscilla, challenge people who say, "Our people don't hike," responding with a loving invitation to see how good God's creation is for the soul and a reminder that just because Western media doesn't show Chinese or Korean people loving the outdoors, there are a billion people who might say otherwise. I know she feels connected to her late Baba on earth and her Father in heaven, and racism isn't going to destroy that. I am in awe every time she refuses to allow prejudice, racism, or stereotypes to keep her from God's good gifts.

Our annual camping and snowboarding trips have become a ritual where good friends and family connect around a campfire or fireplace. As our group pitches tents or strolls through the lodge, we walk in the truth that nowhere in the Bible does God say people of color can't enjoy the water or winter sports.

I have seen families vacation together for decades. Our friends James and Anna Lee-Winans kept their relationships vibrant with tact and intentionality after college. I know walks on the beach, strolls through botanical gardens, or drives to see the leaves change can ground us in much more than a good time. These moments don't require an extraordinary income for an exceptional outcome. What's necessary is the giving of oneself over to receiving and reflecting the love of God and his kingdom in context. When this is done regularly, the fruit of good seeds sown is beauty and resistance.

RESIST

4

what are we resisting?

Therefore, I urge you, brothers and sisters, in view of God's mercy, to offer your bodies as a living sacrifice, holy and pleasing to God—this is your true and proper worship. Do not conform to the pattern of this world, but be transformed by the renewing of your mind. Then you will be able to test and approve what God's will is—his good, pleasing and perfect will.

ROMANS 12:1-2

When I entered a therapist's office for the first time in 2013, I started to take seriously the idea that my emotional and spiritual maturity were inextricably linked. This rang especially true when addressing the most pressing issues of our day, such as racism, economic inequality, and sexual violence. I knew in my head God was calling me to be his disciple and to preach the gospel in word, deed, and power. But what started to work its way into my heart was that God also called me his child. To receive and reflect that reality, it was paramount that I grow in my spiritual and emotional health, awareness, and intelligence. And that was starting to happen.

I was responding to racist comments online with gracious invitations to see things differently. I was naming difficult emotions, identifying destructive narratives, and trying to replace them with practices that modeled the Christ I was getting to know. I was growing—but I did not feel successful. All of my previous formation urged me toward bigger, more, better, faster. And I felt invisible and irrelevant. I was used to fighting battles outside my home, but I did not know how to win those in my heart and household. My activism and resistance normally came in the form of a vigil, petition, protest, boycott, or demonstration. Work done, event over, box checked.

The work of formation never felt complete. But after a key conversation with a friend in the midst of a wave of racial unrest, something shifted.

REBECCA, VICTORIA, AND NOELLE

Rebecca is the mother of two Black sons who lives in a historic Black neighborhood in Washington, DC. I shared with her everything I was experiencing and the tension I felt. She told me she felt no tension at all, because surviving in a world that made no space for her was an act of resistance. And raising two Black sons who know their worth, value, and immovable place at the table of their Father in heaven in the family of God was her protest every day.

Every game they played, prayer she prayed, and meeting she attended to ensure they got all the love and justice they needed was her full-time vocation.

When I walked through her home, I saw mountains of LEGO bricks, dinosaur books, her eldest son's "garden," and numerous pets. Together these intertwined to form an image of beauty and resistance. I accepted the invitation not just to move toward a more holistic orientation around the kingdom of God instead of the patterns of the world, but also to name and frame the deliberate choices I was making in light of the kingdom of God and its inherent opposition to the way our world is organized. I also resolved to appreciate and encourage those who were making similar choices.

Victoria is a racially assigned White woman of German descent who stepped into the pulpit of our church and told the story of her ancestors' service in the Nazi army. She confessed her family's complicity in violence, how she benefits from Whiteness, and her commitment to learning to connect her faith to the fight against White supremacy and racism. This talk was not a high point or culmination but another step in the long walk of obedience to God that continues in places known to us and to her.

Noelle shared with me that she wanted to have a conversation with her father about gun violence but feared his reaction. She was afraid that if she shared her opinions, there would be more distance and the abandonment she had felt as a child would replay for her as an adult. As we talked through the situation, she named her fear, was liberated from her sense of powerlessness, and expressed her desire to have a mature, honest relationship with her father. This dialogue was about gun violence and generational patterns of lies, deceit, and peacekeeping. She was going to lovingly confront that reality and seek Jesus and his kingdom in the midst of it.

Not one of these people would see themselves as activists or participants in any sort of revolution. But I firmly believe they are! To know Jesus and to follow him is to resist the powers and principalities that operate in this world and reflect the kingdom of God and victory of Christ over sin—individual and corporate—in every area of life. Resistance is purposeful, contextualized, loving action informed by prayerful reflection individually and in community.

By God's grace and his power, these women were not operating out of the broken patterns or narratives of dominant culture, their families, or history. Instead, they were resisting them. Godly resistance is the loving, purposeful disruption of patterns of abuse, violence, exploitation, greed, corruption, and every other sin that is at odds with the intended will of God for all of creation. And they were doing just that—one raising children, one in the pulpit, and one at her parent's house receiving and reflecting the kingdom of God.

These were fruitful steps, but they are not easy to imitate or sustain. Once I started to prioritize rest and experiment with different rhythms of restoration, the patterns, narratives, and scripts that led to my burnout in the first place began to resurface. But because I was well fed, well rested, and receiving heavy doses of the love and support of God, my family, and my community, I could respond from a place of wholeness instead of feelings of lack, anxiety, or fear.

I was more able to see where my own will fell short, resist social norms that harmed me, and stand on the promises of God in faith when tempted by the enemy to do otherwise. I meaningfully engaged in the personal and social reality that the United States was established by Europeans who exterminated Native peoples, enslaved Africans, exploited the poor of all ethnic backgrounds, stole land, and extracted resources for the benefit of a few—a pattern that continues today.

The effects of the terrible temptation to see ourselves above and separate from one another and creation instead of integral parts of both persist and must be pushed back against. Colonization, or the remaking of the world into the image of the dominant individual, group, class, country, and ideology, opposes the notion that we are made in the image of God, designed to reflect his image and live in his kingdom. This race, class, gender, and environmental hierarchy rules our segregated and stratified society and enforces assimilation at five levels: individual, intimate, interpersonal, institutional, and ideological.

This would be overwhelming if not for Jesus' initial sermon after being tempted in the desert, the words of the apostle Paul to the early church, and the witness of Rev. Dr. Martin Luther King Jr. Because of Christ, pillars of our faith, and the great cloud of witnesses, I recognize I live in the legacies of many who were able to endure suffering and resist injustice. And I can live out the Great Commission, obey the great commandments, and disciple others to do the same.

THE INVITATION TO FOLLOW JESUS IS AN INVITATION TO A REVOLUTION

I attend New Life Fellowship Church in New York. Traditionally, when someone is baptized in our congregation, we ask them two questions: "Do you choose to follow Jesus as your Lord and Savior?" and "Do you renounce Satan and all his ways?"

If the person being baptized says yes to both of these questions, they are immersed in the water in the name of the Father, Son, and Holy Spirit. Then they are raised to life anew and met with a standing ovation. After raucous applause, we extend our hands in prayerful support while leaders lay hands on those baptized to pray for the filling of the Holy Spirit. Though the account of Pentecost in Acts 2 shows the power of the Holy Spirit when he fell on those gathered in the upper room after Jesus' ascension, our baptisms can seem a little less eventful.

Baptisms today are certainly no less significant, but they can feel less consequential. While they are declarative, they are not often presented as revolutionary. This contrasts sharply with awareness in Jesus' day. Many disciples faced gruesome martyrdom because the arrival of the Messiah and their allegiance to him carried profound social, political, and religious significance. They felt this impact as individuals, families, the Jewish people, privileged and oppressed populations within the Roman Empire, and the Roman Empire itself. The same should be true for us today, and I don't believe that this is happening.

LIKE A BASKETBALL GAME GONE WRONG

Force and conviction are present in many sermons, congregations, conferences, and creeds, but they are misguided and applied in the wrong way. It would be like Hall of Fame basketball player Shaquille O'Neal dunking the ball on the goal he was supposed to defend and breaking the rim and backboard. Shaq broke many rims in his career, most notably during his rookie season with the Orlando Magic in 1993. But never on his own hoop. If this ever happened, spectators would cry out, "What are you doing?" and then Shaq would go to the bench so he wouldn't do that again. And he'd likely get a visit from his stepfather midgame.[1]

But instead of negative consequences for giving the opposing team two points, snapping the momentum, and stopping the game as the rim is repaired, the player is greeted with a chorus of agreement and wild affirmation. "Keep going!" and "You are awesome!" the crowd chants while the announcer whips them into an even greater frenzy.

The NBA has specific protocols for broken rims. They are common sense for a community that desires to accomplish something together—especially to keep everyone safe. According to the rules, play is stopped until the equipment is removed or repaired, and no foul is assessed. But in our twisted scenario, the referees don't pause to give staff time to clean up the broken glass. The crowd's demand for the game to continue is incessant. They tell Shaq and others that this is what they get paid for. The ownership group sends word to the coaches that the game must go on since any sustained pause in the action could dent their profits. So the officials and the players are convinced that to stop would be too costly. They gear up to try to play on the court and the shards. The game continues and a winner is declared as the clock runs out.

The impact of this choice ripples outwards. Instead of being replaced, the broken backboard is replicated. The rules change to cement the reality that one team having a complete backboard and rim while the other plays on shattered glass is good, right, and how God intended. If a historian or layperson later brings up the event as ridiculous given the nature of the game, goals of its founders, and legends of the league, they are either dismissed or, at worst, excommunicated for declaring that what is happening is not how it should be.

This drastic change impacts parents and players in the development pipeline. Because of their materially impoverished backgrounds or positions in the power structure, they alter their training and adopt the narrative. They desperately want to be part of the game. They *need* to be a part of it. Any challenge to what has happened evaporates.

Those unable to change leave. Those who remain and resist are under constant scrutiny, and those who are hurt are shushed or paid for their silence. The game, which has now become a show, must go on. And now it has gone on for so long that it seems everyone has forgotten how to play properly.

FAITH IN WHAT YOU CAN SEE

The Jesus of the Gospel of John, along with the disciples faithful to the Great Commandments and the Great Commission, are like the 2014 NBA champion San Antonio Spurs—arguably one of the greatest teams ever assembled, including four members of the Hall of Fame.[2] There were no superstars, and winning remained the focus. That season they ranked first in field goals, assists, and three-point percentage.[3] Their unselfish and team-oriented style of play was a hallmark of their success and contributed significantly to their eventual championship victory.

Conversely, what most congregants hear on Sunday mornings, watch online, or experience at conferences are preachers and teachers more interested in growing their own platforms, influence, and net worth. Modern depictions of faithfulness make no sense when compared to the preached word and lived life of Jesus, yet there is an entire ecosystem pushing this constructed reality and millions committed to its deception. These institutions and individuals exalt a prosperity gospel antithetical to Jesus, a militarism that contradicts the Sermon on the Mount, and a religious, racial, and gender supremacy that the book of Acts vehemently opposes. These religious leaders have dunked on their own goal and are telling everyone listening to them on podcasts, in pews, or on YouTube to play on broken glass and put a ball through a hoop on the ground.

Hebrews 11:1-7 declares:

> Now faith is confidence in what we hope for and assurance about what we do not see. This is what the ancients were commended for.
>
> By faith we understand that the universe was formed at God's command, so that what is seen was not made out of what was visible.
>
> By faith Abel brought God a better offering than Cain did. By faith he was commended as righteous,

when God spoke well of his offerings. And by faith Abel still speaks, even though he is dead.

By faith Enoch was taken from this life, so that he did not experience death: "He could not be found, because God had taken him away." For before he was taken, he was commended as one who pleased God. And without faith it is impossible to please God, because anyone who comes to him must believe that he exists and that he rewards those who earnestly seek him.

By faith Noah, when warned about things not yet seen, in holy fear built an ark to save his family. By his faith he condemned the world and became heir of the righteousness that is in keeping with faith.

Faith, in the book of Hebrews, is framed as an action springing from a choice to trust God for something that was promised but made no logical sense. God would accomplish it by his power, not because the circumstances allowed it but because he is sovereign over all circumstances. Noah built a boat on dry land, Enoch didn't die when every human is supposed to, and Abel, though killed by Cain, was called righteous by God. The predominant narratives about these individuals could have been the complete opposite—and sometimes they are.

To followers of Jesus, Noah's story is a testimony of faithfulness out of context, but it's ridiculous to imagine someone actually doing it in practice. Abel was faithful, but he's dead, and our dominant narratives around discipleship and formation often drive Christians toward comfort and away from anything contrary or controversial. So our offerings to God are not aligned with Abel's testimony and wholly avoid what happened to him. Put plainly, we praise God in ways that please the powerful and people around us, not God as he has commanded, lest someone send an email, want to meet up, or spread rumors. Finally, everyone dies, so the testimony of Enoch is framed as just a story to encourage us, while few truly believe we could please the God of fire and brimstone enough for him to hold back judgment and give mercy.

It is no wonder that the Jesus who is poor, who abounds in love and justice for those cast aside, and who rose from the dead is rejected by a church that puts a pale-faced, straight-haired, well-dressed version of him in a stained-glass window.

Our current context platforms and protects people and systems that perpetrate and perpetuate violence and inequity or benefit from them. This is true in the Southern Baptist Convention, the Boy Scouts of America, and the police precincts in communities like Ferguson, Missouri, and Minneapolis, Minnesota.[4] The only people from the margins of society who are praised and lifted up by the dominant culture are those who serve or submit to the goals of the dominant culture. Those who "work hard" and are "obedient" are held up as examples. And revolutionary figures are stripped of their views and reintroduced as agents of empire and participants in the hierarchies of dominance.

This is what happened when Jesus of Nazareth became White, American, Christian nationalist, and the moral force behind imperial expansion.

BAPTIZED INTO THE WORLD

Instead of being baptized into the family of God and integrated into the beloved community, many Christians end up following a distorted Jesus with a party, platform, and agenda. We adopt worldly practices and behaviors that, if challenged, make others question Jesus and the gospel. We go down into the waters of baptism as people made in the image of God and rise up as wet Americans primed for faith in nation, not the kingdom of heaven.

The invitation and the command is to put our hope and trust in the world we have made and the work of our hands instead of the word and work of God. If Noah were alive today, most professed Christians would be outside the ark as it began to rain. If this were the time of Enoch, supposed believers would say that surely he left and was not lifted by God to dwell with him. And if Abel and Cain's story happened this year, the focus would be on whether Cain's actions were justifiable, not on Abel's faithful sacrifice.

The hearers of these wonderful accounts from Hebrews were not present when these incidents occurred, but they chose to believe because of their faith in Christ and his promises. The rabbis preached a connection to their Jewish roots and the now ascended Messiah. The hearers had a choice to hear Jesus as he said he was and to believe. We must make the same choice to believe what we have not seen and be blessed as Jesus promised (John 20:29).

The same force that the earliest believers resisted under Roman rule is still at work today. Colonization is a pervasive system that damages humanity's way of being and seeks to permanently reshape them if allowed. To resist this, we rely on the gospel of Jesus Christ and the good news of the kingdom. These are the foundation for standing against forces that seek to assimilate us into a system we were not meant for. By developing individual and communal habits that integrate beauty and resistance through Christ, we can live out the reality of God's kingdom here and now.

IMPLICATIONS OF CONFESSING JESUS IS LORD

When the disciples proclaimed that Jesus is Lord and decided to follow him, they were making a social, political, and religious statement. It was not solely a public acknowledgment that Jesus was their personal Lord and Savior. For the speakers and the hearers, these themes were intertwined and the implications well known. John the Baptist was beheaded, Jesus was crucified, the apostles were in and out of prison. Conversely, many current-day "Christians" have exchanged their faith in Jesus of Nazareth for Jesus of nationalism. This is a fake messiah of White American Folk Religion—a race, class, gender, and environmental hierarchy that places Whiteness, patriarchy, greed, and wealth under a messiah who endorses the imperial project.[5]

Often quoted in modern evangelical spaces is former Netherlands prime minister and Dutch Reformed neo-Calvinist thinker Abraham Kuyper. In his famous speech opening the Free University in 1880, Kuyper said, "There's not a square inch in the whole domain of human existence over which Christ, who is Lord over all, does not exclaim, 'Mine!'"[6] As prime minister Kuyper supported Eurocentric ideas of colonization and imperialism. He held to the idea that Western Christian nations had a responsibility to "civilize" non-Western societies. He viewed Dutch colonialism as part of a divine mandate to bring Christianity and "progress" to other parts of the world, which he saw as underdeveloped or uncivilized. In Kuyper's view, European (particularly Dutch Calvinist) culture was superior, and it was the duty of Europeans to guide and uplift all others for God. What actually happened was an anti-Christian mission of land theft, genocide, enslavement, sexual violence, and environmental destruction at scale.

This perfectly captures the thought patterns behind our tendency to see our beliefs and actions as separate when they are deeply intertwined. Kuyper preached that all people were made in the image of God while supporting divine accumulation of wealth and extraction of resources from people he believed were inherently inferior and a planet he argued was his to possess. Thus the Dutch Reformed Church provided a theological justification for apartheid in South Africa. The apostle James warns about this type of gross hypocrisy, especially for leaders. James 3:1, 9-10 says:

> Not many of you should become teachers, my fellow believers, because you know that we who teach will be judged more strictly. . . .
>
> With the tongue we praise our Lord and Father, and with it we curse human beings, who have been made in God's likeness. Out of the same mouth come praise and cursing. My brothers and sisters, this should not be.

These and many other teachings that call for integrity are disregarded or distorted into justifications for daily intimate and industrial-size atrocities.

Because of this history, much of "Christian" tradition is the fruit of European colonialism and the unholy matrimony of the merchant, the missionary, and the militant. The full-throated, heavy-handed adoption of White American Folk Religion feels ritualistic and religious—but in no way is it "Christian." Reading through the prophet Isaiah's indictments of religious festivals (Isaiah 1:13-15), James's condemnation of favoritism (James 2:9), and Jesus' rebuke of the Pharisees (Matthew 23:13-36), we see that the way of Christ is eternally resistant to hierarchy and domination. But Kuyper, along with his contemporaries and counterparts, embraces segregation and stratification with himself on top.

This is one of many tainted aquifers from which the majority of today's church contexts draw their waters of baptism. Our pastors, congregants, and denominational leaders are downstream and swimming in seas of prejudice, theft, and violence. This is true of every Western denomination, including but not limited to Catholics, Lutherans, Presbyterians, Baptists, and their affiliates via church splits or missions in every corner of the world.

Instead of preaching love, condemning greed, and casting an imaginative vision for kingdom justice to our culture, pastors and leaders seem beholden to the dominant culture. The current is strong and the waters are deep. For those upstream of power structures, it is much easier to go with the flow and seek life, liberty, and the pursuit of happiness rather than take up your cross, deny yourself, and follow Jesus. The current feels too powerful. Fortunately, Jesus is the one who calms storms and seas with a word. If only we would heed his call.

RESISTING THE FLOW IS NOT EASY

It's easier to go with the flow than resist it. And that is my problem. The city I live in, the ministry context where I work, the family I come from, and whom I often spend time with run alongside me toward efficiency, productivity, and accumulation. Memories of events recent and years past form an elaborate tapestry in my mind that tells a story that blankets my reality. I was encouraged, validated, and celebrated at most steps of the way climbing up and over others to get up the ladder.

I write these words mostly late at night after my kids have gone to bed in the city that never sleeps. My surrounding context is one of exceptional wealth made possible by the trading of enslaved people, industrialized products, and re-sources extracted near and far. You are most likely reading these words in a country that measures its value primarily by military might and its gross domestic product or lis-tening to them on a device that costs more than 44 percent of what the world lives off in a month.[7]

My home is on land that colonial powers deemed un-derused, where its indigenous inhabitants were tricked and wiped out to make way for a settler colony serving Dutch and British rulers. The waters upstream of me, my family, my people, and all that I encounter are exceptionally strong, because colonization is a complete, all-encom-passing process.

This is by design. Oppressive ideologies are intact, above, and intertwined with everything—from our beliefs and institutions to our personal relationships and individual thoughts. They are so deeply ingrained in our lives and minds that it's hard to identify them. Even more challenging is to imagine life apart from them. But to identify and imagine is precisely what we must do. And followers of Jesus must do it with discipline, rigor, and regularity to resist seduction, complacency, and resignation. Resistance is core to following Jesus.

THE COLONY VERSUS THE KINGDOM OF GOD

Aníbal Quijano was a prominent Peruvian decolonial sociologist, scholar, and author. His work explored how colonial structures of power, knowledge, and hierarchy shape modern society even after the end of the formal colonial structure. In his famous essay "Coloniality and Modernity," he says:

> The colonizers also imposed a mystified image of their own patterns of producing knowledge and meaning. At first, they placed these patterns far out of reach of the dominated. Later, they taught them in a partial and selective way, in order to co-opt some of the dominated into their own power institutions. Then European culture was made seductive: it gave access to power. After all, beyond repression, the main instrument of all power is its seduction. Cultural Europeanisation was transformed into an aspiration. It was a way of participating and later to reach the same material benefits and the same power as the Europeans: viz. to conquer nature in short for "development." European culture became a universal cultural model. The

imaginary in the non-European cultures could hardly exist today and, above all, reproduce itself outside of these relations.[8]

All that surrounds me in life has been constructed, and for it to undergo the renovation necessary to reflect the kingdom of God and not this world, I must uncouple it from colonial forces at work in plain sight and behind the scenes. As Jesus said, the kingdom of God is like yeast that works its way through an entire batch of dough (Matthew 13:33). Coloniality has worked its way through in five ways and Jesus is working the dough of this world toward a different end. Baptism is a public confession that he has delivered us from this temptation, and our discipleship is how he plans for us to embody that liberation.

Ideology. The first way colonialism legitimizes itself is by developing and spreading an idea. Whiteness and the idea of White supremacy are made up. The same is true for capitalism, socialism, communism, and patriarchy. Colonialism would label its ideology as right and all others as wrong—inferior, inhumane, or evil.

The prayers we pray, books we read, Scriptures we memorize, and liturgies we practice deeply form us. Since 2013, I have prayed the same three prayers daily. The Lord's Prayer, the Prayer of Saint Francis, and the Franciscan Benediction orient my heart and mind away from selfishness, prejudice, and greed and pull me toward God's kingdom and his righteousness. It is difficult to pursue the American dream and all it offers if I set my heart's compass daily toward Christ as king.

I chose these three because the Lord's Prayer centers me on God, the Prayer of Saint Francis orients me to others, and the Franciscan Benediction reminds me of the kingdom of God and Jesus' active invitation to be a part of it. The music we listen to and the media feeds we follow can conform us to the patterns of the world or transform us in Christ. Choosing to contemplate, meditate, pray, and intercede individually and collectively is the bedrock of transformative resistance.

Three Prayers

THE LORD'S PRAYER

Our Father which art in heaven, Hallowed be thy name.
Thy kingdom come, Thy will be done in earth, as it is
in heaven.
Give us this day our daily bread.
And forgive us our debts, as we forgive our debtors.
And lead us not into temptation, but deliver us from evil:
For thine is the kingdom, and the power, and the glory,
for ever. Amen. (Matthew 6:9-13 KJV)

THE PRAYER OF SAINT FRANCIS

Lord, make me an instrument of your peace.
Where there is hatred, let me sow love.
Where there is injury, pardon.

Where there is doubt, faith.

Where there is despair, hope.

Where there is darkness, light.

And where there is sadness, joy.

Oh Divine Master, grant that I may not so much seek to be
consoled as to console,

to be understood as to understand.

To be loved as to love.

For it is in giving that we receive.

It is in pardoning that we are pardoned.

And it is in dying that we are born to eternal life. Amen.

THE FRANCISCAN BENEDICTION

May God bless you with discomfort at easy answers,
half-truths, and superficial relationships so that you may
live deeply in your heart.

May God bless you with tears to shed for those who suffer
pain, rejection, hunger, and war so that you may reach out
your hand to comfort them and turn their pain to joy.

May God bless you with righteous anger at injustice,
oppression and exploitation of people and the planet that
you may work for justice, freedom, and peace.

And may God bless you with enough foolishness to
believe that you can make a difference in the world.

So that you can do what others claim cannot be done.

To bring justice, kindness, and the good news of Jesus to
all people—especially to children and the poor. Amen.

Institutions. Ideologies permeate society through institutions. Financial, educational, government, military,

theological, and social systems and structures are the mechanisms that practice, defend, and enforce the ideologies of a given people. In coloniality, institutions are the largest levers for enforcing hierarchies of dominance, and every rule, law, ordinance, and bureaucratic decision serves the pleasure, comfort, and preference of the dominant culture. Conversely, these institutions discriminate, marginalize, and actively minimize and undermine the interests of people and people groups they determine should be subjugated.

There are companies, businesses, and organizations that I refuse to support and actively oppose because of their impact on marginalized people. Whenever possible, I buy fair-trade goods like chocolate, sugar, coffee, and clothing. Our family does our best not to support churches or nonprofits that choose to hold up systems we believe are detrimental to God's purposes in the world. We go to the polls as a family and talk through how and why we support the candidates we do at the local, state, and national level. All of these things and more serve to resist the lie that we are hopeless, helpless, and incapable of making this world more loving, just, beautiful, and kind.

Moreover, within the institutions where we work and have influence, we use our authority to reflect the kingdom of God as best we can through pursuing equitable pay for folks we hire, and we press for justice and equity when it comes to women, people of color, the disabled, and other marginalized people.

Interpersonal. For ideas to have power, institutions must implement them. And for institutions to be effective, they need people willing to participate in them and exercise those beliefs as they interact with people in public spaces.

It is not the idea of police brutality that killed George Floyd or Breonna Taylor; it was officers and representatives of our legal system along the chain of command that participated in those murders. It was not Congress that implemented the Chinese Exclusion Act or Franklin Delano Roosevelt's Executive Order 9066 that interned one hundred twenty thousand Japanese Americans. There were soldiers, officials, and community members willing and able to collaborate with one another to perpetrate injustice and follow unjust orders.

When I make deliberate choices about my personal life—how I address those who serve my food, deliver my groceries, or attend my house of worship—I can be complicit or resistant to ideas and institutions. The gospel calls us to resist conformity, say no to crushing the image of God in those around us, and pursue shalom with all of creation. "Love your neighbor as yourself" is a revolutionary command in a society that says to hide, hoard, and be afraid of them. God made us for community that prioritizes every individual, not institutions that minimize individuals to protect themselves. If Christ-followers modeled this community, then those who desired to leave institutions would have a people and a place to go to.

Intimacies. Ideas and institutions don't just operate in public but also in private. Who we marry, how we raise our children, how we make decisions about what we eat, drink, and wear behind closed doors—all of these are influenced by ideologies, implemented by institutions, and enforced by people willing to participate in public and private spaces. Scholars Erika Perez and Anne Marie Plane call these spaces "colonial intimacies." In these private spaces, parents, relatives, caretakers, and other "custodians of colonialism" ensure that ideas around race, class, gender, and environment are mastered and passed on to the next generation.[9]

With this in mind, I resist enforcing patriarchy, dominance, and cultural superiority within the walls of my home—as best as I possibly can—with the words I say, actions I take, and posture I have every day. If I make a mistake, I must be willing to confess, repent, and seek reconciliation. I am not perfect, because for decades this was not my mindset or focused intention. But prayer, Scripture, and reflection have sprouted seeds in me that have yielded fruits of the Spirit because I have chosen orientation to God, others, and his kingdom—not patriarchy, hierarchy, or fake strength masking my own fragility.

Individual. Once ideas have worked their way through society, culture, and families by these and other means, an individual doesn't need systems or people to function accordingly. Individuals police themselves and adhere to accepted patterns and practices because they fear the consequences, they hold genuine conviction of their own rightness, or they are resigned to the belief that things will never change.

For me, it is perhaps hardest to break away from the deformation of White American Folk Religion and reflect the life of Jesus when no one is around. Without my wife or daughters in view or earshot, will I choose to objectify women via pornography or social media? Will I use my money to gamble or make secret purchases for the dopamine hit? Will I drink too much or pop a pill to take the edge off for a bit? The answer isn't always no. But instead of cycling down the toilet bowl of condemnation and worthlessness, I remember the liturgy I share with my kids, the truth of Romans 8, and the power of the gospel. I resist alignment with the false ideology that I can be loved and accepted only if I am obedient and compliant. And I receive the love of God that was meant for me from the beginning.

To engage this high and wide scope of brokenness can be overwhelming. Yet this is the context Jesus lived in, preached to, pushed back against, and overcame. This full reality is the one that crucified him and the one he called home. Those who were obedient to his teachings and filled with the Spirit supported and taught one another. And their witness encourages and compels followers today. So it is my deep privilege to enter into that tradition and seek out how Jesus is calling me, my family, and the communities and institutions where I have authority and influence under the banner of Jesus as Lord. The gospel is good news to all people at all times, delivered and received with their unique realities in mind. We see this when Jesus chooses to use parables and imagery, healing and miracles to reach those around him.

I also believe that if we live in the aftermath of a colonial structure where hierarchy and dominance permeate every sector of life, then the kingdom of God must bring liberation, love, and justice to every place. Kuyper was right that God looks out and says, "Mine!" But instead of looking to dominate and extract, God looks to bring his love, sacrifice, and justice to all people, not a few. He says "mine" because he shaped all of us in our mothers' wombs (Psalm 139:13-14), desires that none of us perish (2 Peter 3:8-9), and wants all people to be reconciled to him (2 Corinthians 5:18-21).

JESUS' FIRST SERMON IN CONTEXT

Jesus lived a life of integrity—from individual to ideological. At the beginning of Luke 4, after Jesus was filled with the Holy Spirit, he was taken to the desert to be tempted. After forty days of fasting, the devil tempted him with three things: provision, power, and protection. Jesus was hungry, so for the first temptation, the enemy told him to make bread. What Jesus knew in his heart and mind to be true he stood upon to resist an ideological frame of reference. Jesus knew who he was and *whose* he was, so he could stand.

Next, Jesus was materially impoverished and from Nazareth—a small town on the wrong side of the tracks. Moreover, Jesus was a Palestinian Jewish carpenter born out of wedlock. His family and entire people group suffered under the brutal occupation of the Roman Empire. So Satan promised him power to leave that behind and rule over those who ruled over him. If Jesus chose this path, it would put him atop the hierarchy and let him dictate the intimacies of life and dynamics of interpersonal relationships, and give him rule over institutions. Again, though, Jesus pushed back because he knew his kingdom was not of this world, and, again, the guiding factor for the enemy was self-interest. Jesus' priority was the Father's business (Luke 2:41-49).

Last, Satan knew that Jesus could command angels to protect him, so the enemy told him to jump off a peak in Jerusalem. Again, Jesus was consistent in thought and action and demonstrated integrity in his response. In these three instances Jesus resisted with Scripture. Later he resisted with words and action through his preaching and his ministry, inviting people to step into a different ideological, institutional, interpersonal, and intimate reality. One not governed by oppressive religious and political leaders, exploitative cultural norms, or hierarchical relationships inside and outside the home.

Jesus preached his first sermon in his hometown and announced his ministry by quoting Isaiah 61. Luke 4:16-21 says this:

> [Jesus] went to Nazareth, where he had been brought up, and on the Sabbath day he went into the synagogue, as was his custom. He stood up to read, and the scroll of the prophet Isaiah was handed to him. Unrolling it, he found the place where it is written:
> "The Spirit of the Lord is on Me,
>> because he has anointed me
>> to proclaim good news to the poor.
> He has sent me to proclaim freedom for the prisoners
>> and recovery of sight for the blind,
> to set the oppressed free,
>> to proclaim the year of the Lord's favor."
> Then he rolled up the scroll, gave it back to the attendant and sat down. The eyes of everyone in the synagogue were fastened on him. He began by saying to them, "Today this scripture is fulfilled in your hearing."

Moreover, the apostle Paul said in Ephesians 6:12, "Our struggle is not against flesh and blood, but against the rulers, against the authorities, against the powers of this dark world and against the spiritual forces of evil in the heavenly realms."

Jesus said no to the enemy and no to the temptations of this world to be deceived by wealth, the worries of this world, and the desires for other things (Mark 4:18-19). He demonstrated his love for us and gave an example to emulate, along with the power to do even greater things (John 14:12-14).

BEAUTY AND RESISTANCE ARE EMBODIED INTEGRITY

In 2 Corinthians 5, we learn that we are Christ's ambassadors and have been given the ministry of reconciliation. In Acts 1 we read that we will be his witnesses. It is difficult to be an ambassador when we don't know the message we are bringing, and we would be hard-pressed to be effective witnesses if we didn't behold the Father, Son, and Spirit with regularity. Practically speaking, it is difficult to resist racism and White supremacy if I am not regularly contemplating my adoption into the family of God. I find it hard to truly be open to learning and not defensive in conversations about patriarchy and masculinity if I am not reflecting on the reality that I do not have to dominate, control, or appear superior in every situation.

If I am not rested and restored, I will choose comfort and convenience through being nonconfrontational, stress eating, and cutting corners on the practices that make my life and household more sustainable for the planet. I will center my own needs over those of others and show the type of favoritism and selfishness Jesus' brother James warns against in his epistle to the early church. Just like Jesus, I will find myself tempted by my own desires, the way of the world, and the enemy, but unlike him, I won't be able to turn away.

That is, unless I build a life that allows me to experience the joy of the Lord and give and receive his love in ever-increasing measure. I must build a life around Christ in my context, which is much like his. But since I am not starting from scratch, I need scaffolding. Internal and external thoughts, actions, and patterns will need to change for me and my community to reflect in our hearts and in the world the renewal Jesus has accomplished.

BUILDING A HOME

My wife and I own a home in New York City. But it is not the first home we lived in here. When I first committed to campus ministry, I lived in a home on the Upper West Side while raising support for my salary and programming budget. In her later growing-up years Priscilla lived in Queens with a front yard and a driveway. Both of these homes were regularly full of people who did not live there. Sometimes they were full of people living there for a season. The common thread for Priscilla's parents and the family that took me in was that these homes were not theirs but God's. This was not just an aspiration but an experience.

Their names may have been on the mortgages, but these homes did not exist solely for their pleasure, safety, and opportunity to join a good school district. They were set up in such a way that memories could be made for holidays and traditions kept for their families and neighbors made in the image of God. Food was plentiful because guests were welcome, and extra linens were clean because they needed to be ready to take people in. These families did not function as though they had achieved the American dream but lived as though they had been given a tool for God's glory.

Priscilla's childhood friends, church folks she grew up with, and family members talk about meals shared, Scriptures studied, and holidays celebrated around their big dining room table. That circular table is now in our dining room, where new memories are being made and the gospel of Jesus is preached. In the same way a family made space for me, we offer our basement and bedrooms to followers of Jesus committed to ministry and others who need safe places to heal, delight, and taste and see that the Lord is good.

The radical hospitality displayed in the book of Acts is what we want to offer in our home, because our God is one who welcomes. Society suggests the opposite and sets itself up to enforce borders and boundaries, even though if the Sermon on the Mount were practiced, these boundaries would not exist.

For followers of Jesus, our highest aspiration is not to have pleasure and ease for *ourselves* and our families at the ultimate cost to *them* and the environment. These are not signs that the kingdom of God has come; they are marks of conformity to the current system of colossal inequality. They are evidence of individuals and institutions beholden to a collective false self.

Mother Teresa said, "God does not create poverty; we do because we do not share." She is right, and the proper response is repentance through joining God in the renewal of all things and a resistance that permeates every level of our lives. In my life this looks like contemplation, prayerful action, and hospitality as protest through demonstration that another way of being in the world is possible.

The truthful and tragic reality is that White American Folk Religion and coloniality are highly organized, widely practiced, and ever adaptive. So the love and justice of God lived out in the world must be even more persistent, determined, and fiercely kind. God made the world and it was broken by sin. Colonization and imperialists built the world around us, and their ideas and institutions sustain its results. The kingdom of God and followers of Jesus must push back in love and kindness with the same rigor and revolutionary determination with lives scaffolded for beauty and resistance, not oppression and dominance. This revolution is not one we will see on television—not because the media isn't paying attention, but because it takes place in our hearts in regular encounters with God and communities of love.

REPEAT

scaffolding for a life of beauty and resistance

The sabbatical I took from July 2019 to September 2020 certainly changed my life, but all of those changes proved to be fragile and reversible. The forces in the world that pushed me toward burnout had not weakened but intensified. In March 2020, my wife was nine months pregnant, and we had no idea what awaited us in this birthing journey. There are no pre-baby classes for how to manage having a baby in the midst of a pandemic.

On March 17, 2020, New York City shut down the subways, and less than a week later we headed into the hospital amid shadows of uncertainty. While we were there, they stopped allowing fathers into the delivery rooms, and the fathers who were inside couldn't leave. I remember asking if I could go downstairs to get a meal. The nurses looked at each other, trying to come to an agreement without speaking before answering me. These were frightening times.

We left the hospital twenty-four hours earlier than expected because of the pending lockdown, and we saw a line of cars outside. Dads holding cell phones stared up at big windows trying to be supportive to birthing moms high above the pavement. The isolation, grief, and uncertainty were overwhelming.

From the time our daughter was born to the end of that year, more than thirty-five thousand people died from Covid-19 in New York, and more than three hundred died on one day in Queens.[1] The sound of sirens was unceasing, and at 7 p.m. daily, for what never felt long enough, we banged pots and pans to show support for frontline workers. It was clear we were trying to conjure up strength amid so much weakness. And that was just one crisis of 2020.

Police shootings, Asian hate, and the Covid-19 pandemic were in full swing for everyone. Ecclesiastes 3:1 articulates in an eternally relevant way that every season has a beginning and an ending, and when my sabbatical ended, I wanted to be less frenetic and anxious. I wanted to live a responsive life grounded in the values I held most dear, not the latest trend or current frustration. Yet when I reentered my job, logged back into Instagram, and took down my automatic reply, I had every opportunity to get back on the plantation I had worked so hard to leave behind.

The transforming, liberative power of the gospel applied to my current reality. I believed that and still do. But with my times of spiritual direction coming to an end and intense therapy about to change to a different schedule, I had to put people, patterns, and practices in place to ensure that the work I'd done in the past year wasn't undone by how I'd lived for over three decades.

With the changes of every season, and especially after setbacks, I must be crystal clear about the forces driving me toward an individual and collective life with God, others, and the self I want to be. Simultaneously, I must know and engage with internal and external factors driving me away from that goal. A scaffold helps me put into practice the things I was taught and provides supports to hold me together. At some point when learning to ride a bike, the hand on the back of the seat goes away. That time came for me at the end of my sabbatical, and I teetered like a kid who'd just realized the stabilizing hand was not there. I had to take responsibility over my own spiritual, emotional, and mental health journey. I was counting the cost because I was forced to, and now it was time to build. Lewin's force field is a tool that helped me begin that process.

LEWIN'S FORCE FIELD

Lewin's force field analysis, developed by psychologist Kurt Lewin in the 1940s, is a model used to understand and analyze the factors that influence a situation, particularly in the context of organizational change.[2] The model views any given situation as being in equilibrium, maintained by two sets of opposing forces, driving forces and restraining forces:

Driving forces. These are factors that push toward change. They include things like new technologies, competition, changing consumer preferences, and leadership that encourages innovation.

Restraining forces. These are factors that resist change. They include things like employee resistance, organizational culture, fear of the unknown, and existing policies or regulations.

According to Lewin's theory, change occurs when the driving forces outweigh the restraining forces, disrupting the current equilibrium. To successfully implement change, an organization needs to strengthen the driving forces or weaken the restraining forces.

The force field analysis is often depicted as a diagram with the current state in the middle, driving forces on one side, and restraining forces on the other, each represented by arrows (see figure 1).[3] The length or thickness of the arrows can indicate the strength of each force. This visual tool helps leaders and managers identify which factors need to be addressed to move toward a desired change.

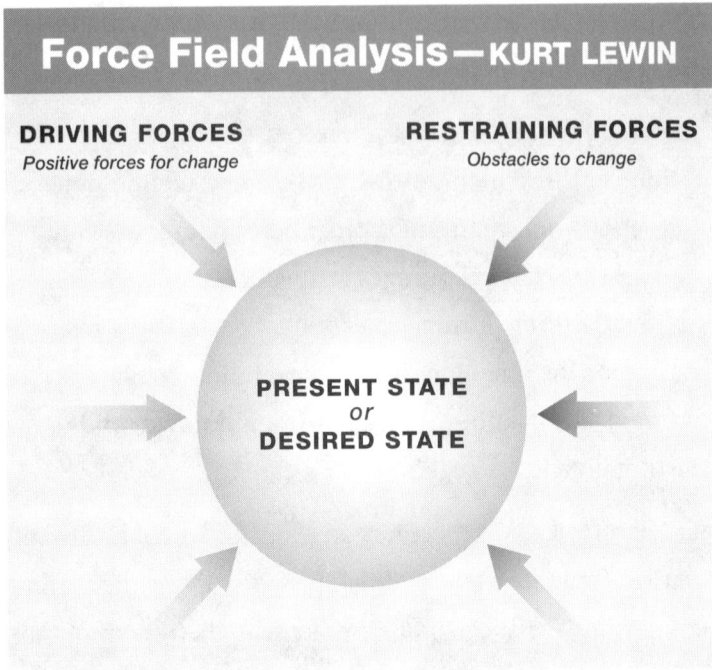

Figure 1. Kurt Lewin's force field analysis

When I was introduced to this tool, it was clear that it was not just for managers looking at organizations or CEOs analyzing businesses. It was for me as I looked at my family and my soul. Clearly, things could not stay the way they were, and that was a felt reality. My feelings, though, were signals for what I believed and valued. They pointed to deeper truths, a broader reality, and my core pursuits. They did not have the fortitude, foresight, or energy to drive me through to the end. I had a bit more work to do.

Remember my Miro board? It had a clear goal. I wanted to live a life that prioritized loving God, myself, and my neighbors nearby and worldwide. I knew I had to begin with the neighbors in my house—my wife and children. I knew my individual, group, and marriage counseling sessions grieved me, but I could not sustain pursuit of my values on regret, guilt, and shame. Yes, the Greatest Commandment—love the Lord with all your heart, soul, mind, and strength and your neighbor as yourself—moved front and center, but I had not defined what was keeping me in the cope-medicate-crash doom loop and what would keep me grounded in the gospel. The dosage of an occasional prayer time, a sermon on Sunday, and an action step that was nonspecific to me were woefully insufficient treatment for the sickness from which I suffered.

I had to reflect on what the life, death, and resurrection of Jesus Christ delivered me and all of creation from. I had to define my context, and coloniality is the spirit of the age that must be thrown down. White American Folk Religion is the power and principality of today. And race, class, gender, and environmental hierarchy under a mock messiah must be left behind. The greed, hypocrisy, and lust for power and control from the ideological to individual levels had to be placed in my personal, familial, communal, geographical, and historical context. With all of these things laid out, I could come to Lewin's force field and ask God to accomplish in me this longing of my heart. Philippians 4:4-9 says this:

Rejoice in the Lord always. I will say it again: Rejoice! Let your gentleness be evident to all. The Lord is near. Do not be anxious about anything, but in every situation, by prayer and petition, with thanksgiving, present your requests to God. And the peace of God, which transcends all understanding, will guard your hearts and your minds in Christ Jesus.

Finally, brothers and sisters, whatever is true, whatever is noble, whatever is right, whatever is pure, whatever is lovely, whatever is admirable—if anything is excellent or praiseworthy—think about such things. Whatever you have learned or received or heard from me, or seen in me—put it into practice. And the God of peace will be with you.

I desperately wanted to rejoice and be emotionally present to those around me. This required that I mourn as well, because to rejoice fully, I would have to acknowledge the pain and devastation I usually avoid. I desired to be gentle with myself and others as a result of my growth in vulnerability and emotional sensitivity.

I desired not to have my life be overrun by fear and anxiety but instead to press into the presence of God to ask for what I needed so I could receive his love, experience his joy, and live into the intertwined beauty and resistance for which I was saved. I wanted to dwell and meditate on the things of God and then act on what is pure, admirable, right, loving, and excellent in my day and age for all people instead of doomscrolling and escaping through technology with my thoughts and actions dictated by an algorithm attuned for perpetual outrage or epic distraction.

Lewin's force field would help me move from imagination to embodiment by providing a structure to define my current and desired context. This would be sandwiched between the individual, intimate, interpersonal, institutional, and ideological forces that pressed me toward or pushed me away. Once completed, I would have a picture of what would make freedom and integrity possible and what would destroy it.

Table 2. Questions to ask in a force field analysis

Driving Forces	Desired Goal	Restraining Forces
Ideological: What do I believe to be true?		**Ideological:** What am I tempted to believe is real?
Institutional: What systems and structures keep those ideas in place?		**Institutional:** What systems and structures support what I am tempted to believe?
Interpersonal: Who are the people who reinforce these thoughts, feelings, and actions?	**Example:** I want to live a life that prioritizes loving God, myself, and my neighbor.	**Interpersonal:** Who are the people who challenge the thoughts and feelings I desire to have?
Intimate: Who are the people immediately around me, and what are the norms they encourage and enforce?		**Intimate:** Who are the people immediately around me, and what are the norms they reward and punish?
Individual: What patterns of thought, feeling, and action in my inner life would orient me toward this desired outcome?		**Individual:** What patterns of thought, feeling, and action in my inner life would orient me away from this desired outcome?

Here are my responses at this stage in life:

Ideological driving forces. I believe in the core of my being that Jesus loves me and the entirety of all creation with an abounding, overflowing, bottomless well of affection. I believe we were made to be in just, loving, and harmonious relationships with one another at all times in every place. I believe that this was, is, and has already been his will and that he demonstrated it through the testimony of his life, death, and resurrection. I believe I and all people were made in his image to follow him.

Ideological restraining forces. The restraining force is the false gospel that would tell me otherwise. Instead of God being liberator, he is the master of the universal plantation seated atop a hierarchy of domination where we seek to earn his favor by fulfilling our place in the structure and crushing other people to move to a more desirable place. Instead of abundance there is scarcity and instead of grace there is ceaseless effort to maintain my position and keep those I love and the things I own from suffering and violence.

Institutional driving forces. The church propels me upward and onward toward my goal of living out Jesus' Great Commandment. By "church" I don't mean a building, a specific denomination, or a leader with a large social media following. I mean the global body of believers who proclaim that Jesus is Lord and seek to live out his gospel through their books, podcasts, newsletters, songs, organizational work, and faithful acts no one will see. Their testimonies along with the great cloud of witnesses show me that another world is possible as they reflect God's kingdom in their communities.

Institutional restraining forces. At the same time, the greatest restraining forces in my life also come from the "church." By this I mean religious institutions that mask oppression and atrocity with a veneer of Christianity. Reading, seeing, hearing, and personally experiencing ideas that dominate, segregate, and stratify in the name of a conquering Christ push me to despair and desperation. From the justification of the enslavement of Africans and the genocide of Native Americans to the theological defense of apartheid in South Africa to Christian Zionism's unwavering support for the ethnic cleansing of Palestine and the genocide of the Palestinian people—the list is global, wide-ranging, and comprehensive.[4] A quote often attributed to acclaimed author and ethicist James Baldwin says, "I don't believe what you say, because I see what you do." Moreover, anticolonial activist Mahatma Gandhi said:

> I like your Christ, but not your Christianity. . . . I believe in the teachings of Christ, but you on the other side of the world do not, I read the Bible faithfully and see little in Christendom that those who profess faith pretend to see. The Christians above all others are seeking after wealth. Their aim is to be rich at the expense of their neighbors. They come among aliens to exploit them for their own good and cheat them to do so. Their prosperity is far more essential to them than the life, liberty, and happiness of others. The Christians are the most warlike people.[5]

This captures the spirit of a principality wholly opposed to God's will and work in the world that endures today.

Interpersonal driving forces. I believe I have things to offer and that my presence is a gift to others. I don't have to perform for God to see me as valuable and worthy, so I don't have to perform for others for approval or acceptance either. I can speak, share, and listen freely because in the family of God I don't have to prove anything or be exceptional to hold my place. I can share my genuine thoughts, feelings, and struggles with siblings and extended family. I can answer honestly when someone asks, "How are you?" in a checkout line, at church, or at our kitchen counter. I can be myself and that is enough. Walking in that lovability is beautiful, difficult, and worth it.

Interpersonal restraining forces. The primary resistance in my relationships comes from me seeing myself as a tool. When I fall into that mindset, I start treating others the same way. Early in our marriage, Priscilla pointed out that I didn't have any friends outside of work. Once the joint work stopped, so did the relationships. At events where I'm just an observer—like parties or casual gatherings—I struggle to "be myself." If I'm not talking about work or a project, I quickly lose interest and become disengaged, showing little curiosity about others or openness about myself. I can become judgmental and condescending, focused only on fixing the problems I hear. And when I do show curiosity, it's because I believe the person has something I need to solve my own issues.

Intimate driving forces. The dominant driving force toward a life of loving God, my neighbors, and myself in an intimate setting is threefold. When I think of my children growing into adults and not knowing that I love them, that God loves them, and that I would give my life for them to know the meaning of both of those truths, I feel distressed. When I think of my wife not experiencing healing and wholeness in our relationship and not knowing in her bones how much I love her, I am grieved. There is no other place than in our home where that should be more profoundly known. And finally, when I think of never hearing or seeing the delight on their faces when they feel seen, heard, or felt in a conversation, after receiving a gift or reading a book, I am undone. This faithful obedience through kind and gentle love in the mundane moments of life are profound and healing. And they ground me.

Intimate restraining forces. The restraining forces that push back against all of that are deep insecurities. I carry narratives that say I am unqualified and undeserving of the life I have as well as a persistent belief that it could all evaporate because of my genogram. When I live out of the lie that I am destined to repeat the worst parts of my family's history, I lose the best part of myself and miss the precious moments around me each day. When I believe I must earn my keep as a father and husband, that I am being evaluated moment by moment and there is no chance for me to reach the goal of acceptance, I lose precisely what I am working for.

Individual driving forces. When I think of myself and
the profound healing that has happened because I believe
I am worthy of love and belonging, I want more of that.
The fruits of giving myself over to vulnerability have been
immeasurably more than I could ask, think, or imagine.
To feel loved and accepted when I look in the mirror and
believe it at the same time is a gift.

Individual restraining forces. The core restraining force
here is the anti-trinity of my flesh, the world, and the devil.
The enemy desires to destroy me. Full stop. The spiritual
forces of this world that are against Jesus are against me.
And I feel them most acutely when I am alone. During
times of prayer in community and in solitude I have felt,
seen, and been told of demons around me. It is frightening
and would be debilitating if not for the reality that greater
is he that is in me than he that is in the world (1 John 4:4)
and the light of Christ shall not be overcome by any
darkness (John 1:1-5).

Moreover, the patterns of this world and of coloniality
maintain that Black men are disposable, inherently inferior,
and beastly—not human. This lie is reinforced by the media
and my own experiences of racism, bigotry, and the preva-
lence of the "White imaginary," a worldview in which the
presence, perspectives, and experiences of White Americans, especially males of European descent, are treated as
"normal" and the default.[6] Because of how society has been
constructed, the very eyes I see myself with are covered by

anti-Blackness. The gospel has delivered me from that condemnation, but like the blind man healed by Jesus in John 9, I need to have my eyes washed because I cannot see myself or the world as it is and as he made it. Some days I see only the false construction and my flesh—or, more appropriately, my will is too de-formed to embrace the kingdom.

ASSESSING MY ECOSYSTEM

Using Lewin's force field in this way uncovers what is hidden in the shadows and drags it into the light to be seen. There are spiritual forces at work, for and against my flourishing. There are ideas circulating around me, and just like pebbles tossed into a pool, they ripple out into every area of my life if I give them time and space. If I am to live an integrated life that embodies the liberation afforded to me by the work of Jesus on the cross, I must interrogate my life and pursue faithful integration. I am not engaging in self-reflection to find flaws, cast judgment, or condemn myself or others; I am to looking to abide and connect with the true vine:

> "I am the true vine, and my Father is the gardener. He cuts off every branch in me that bears no fruit, while every branch that does bear fruit he prunes so that it will be even more fruitful. You are already clean because of the word I have spoken to you. Remain in me, as I also remain in you. No branch can bear fruit by

itself; it must remain in the vine. Neither can you bear fruit unless you remain in me.

"I am the vine; you are the branches. If you remain in me and I in you, you will bear much fruit; apart from me you can do nothing. If you do not remain in me, you are like a branch that is thrown away and withers; such branches are picked up, thrown into the fire and burned. If you remain in me and my words remain in you, ask whatever you wish, and it will be done for you. This is to my Father's glory, that you bear much fruit, showing yourselves to be my disciples." (John 15:1-8)

God is a gardener, pruning me toward fruitfulness. Except in this case, the fruit is not an apple but the trunk itself. When loggers are harvesting trees, they desire to cut through a log and find no knots. To achieve this, as the tree grows, arborists cut off branches to prevent areas of weakness from forming and stop potential entry points for pests and diseases. When the log reaches the mill and the saw goes through, there is a knot-free arrangement of rings from the heart to the outer bark. My fervent desire is that if someone were to cut into the trunk of my life, like a high-quality log, it would be solid all the way down. That from my thoughts, feelings, and actions when I'm alone all the way through to how I interact with and perceive society, there would be integrity and the ingredients for a life that is well-built.

The words that filled the columns of my force field analysis (see table 3) were able to come forth because of the skills I'd been taught by people who love and care for me and the community that provided a sacred space to be pruned, to learn, and to grow. I am exceedingly grateful, because I feel less like a tree among trees than a stump among redwoods— a stump that received lifesaving nutrients to rejoin the forest.

Table 3. Completed force field analysis

Driving Forces	Desired Goal	Restraining Forces
Ideological: I believe in the core of my being that Jesus loves me and all creation with an abounding, overflowing, bottomless well of affection. I believe we were made to be in just, loving, and harmonious relationships with one another at all times in every place.		**Ideological:** The restraining force is a false gospel that portrays God as a domineering master atop a hierarchical structure where people strive to earn favor through subservience and oppression of others.
Institutional: The church is the global body of believers who proclaim Jesus as Lord and seek to live out his gospel through their books, podcasts, newsletters, songs, organizational work, and faithful acts no one will see.		**Institutional:** Religious institutions mask oppression and atrocity with a veneer of Christianity. Reading, seeing, hearing, and personally experiencing ideas that dominate, segregate, and stratify in the name of a conquering Christ pushes me to despair and desperation.
Interpersonal: I believe I do have things to offer and that my mere presence is a gift to other people. I don't have to perform for God to see me as valuable and worthy, so I don't have to perform for others to approve or accept me either.	**Example:** I want to grow in my awareness of God's love and acceptance of me and communicate that with people around me.	**Interpersonal:** The primary resistance in my relationships comes from seeing myself as a tool. When I fall into that mindset, I start treating others the same way.
Intimate: When I contemplate the beauty and wonder experienced by my wife and children when they know the love and acceptance of God through my words and actions, I feel grounded and strong.		**Intimate:** I believe the lie that I am destined to live out the worst parts of my genogram with my own wife and children. I will be a failure and disappointment no matter what I do.
Individual: I contemplate my own belovedness and inherent acceptance as a child of God in all of my strengths and weaknesses.		**Individual:** I believe lies because of my own insecurities, White supremacy, and anti-Blackness.

FRUITFUL TO CONTRIBUTE, NOT
FAVORED TO CONSUME

I must reassert that this desire for integrity and fruitfulness, for freedom and flourishing, is communal, not individual. Like a solitary tree, I might believe the prevailing assumption that I exist independently, but in reality my survival is bound up with the forest. For as Romans 15:1-6 says:

> We who are strong ought to bear with the failings of the weak and not to please ourselves. Each of us should please our neighbors for their good, to build them up. For even Christ did not please himself but, as it is written: "The insults of those who insult you have fallen on me." For everything that was written in the past was written to teach us, so that through the endurance taught in the Scriptures and the encouragement they provide we might have hope.
>
> May the God who gives endurance and encouragement give you the same attitude of mind toward each other that Christ Jesus had, so that with one mind and one voice you may glorify the God and Father of our Lord Jesus Christ.

Those around me with strength gave of themselves to hold me up and together. Their faith, time, and energy ensured my survival, and now that I have survived, I must not look ahead to see who I can pass on the ladder of significance. I must look down to see who is struggling on the rungs this world has greased to cause them to fall. I have received deeply, so I give as was given to me. The time will come again when I will need to receive from them.

For the longest time, scientists thought plants did not communicate and certainly did not consciously cultivate or care for one another. The default scientific conclusion across the plant and animal kingdom was that competition is the natural state and survival of the fittest rules.[7] But scientists are discovering that there is more cooperation than they had realized. Neil deGrasse Tyson said this in a reel that crossed my Instagram feed:

> When a tree is cut down in the forest, other trees reach out to the victim with their root tips, and send life-saving sustenance, water, sugar, and other nutrients via the mycelium. This continuous IV drip from neighboring trees can keep the stump alive for decades, and even centuries. And they don't only do it for their own kind. They do it for the trees of other species. Why? Is it because they know that their lives depend on the health of the whole forest? And even on beings very different from themselves? Is it possible that trees can think in longer terms than we do?[8]

This concept came from the book *The Hidden Life of Trees* by Peter Wohlleben.[9] In this work Wohlleben, a German forester, explores the interconnectedness of trees and how they support each other, particularly through underground fungal networks (mycelium). The book highlights the surprising ways trees cooperate and form intricate networks, challenging our traditional views of nature as solely competitive.

In a similar way, humanity, though force-fed a diet of self-reliance and bootstrap theology,[10] must recognize that independence is simply not what we were made for. Interdependence, beloved community, and shalom were and are God's goal and intention.

CRAFTING A RULE OF LIFE

So it is with all of this in my heart, mind, and hands that I come to craft a rule of life for beauty and resistance with spiritual rhythms of individual and collective formation and repair under the rule and reign of Jesus—one that stands as a witness to the holistic, transformative power of the gospel. And one planted firmly, wholly against a dominant culture of ideologies and institutions that seek to dominate, exploit, extract, and dispose of people and resources under a false gospel from a fake Jesus that is good news to no one.

With the help of Lewin's force field, I've identified the personal and communal forces driving and restraining me and can discern how to express my call to follow Jesus in my specific context. I can start building the necessary scaffolding around my life to sustain this reorientation, even—especially—when difficulty and opposition arise, and I can truly experience what much of Christian teaching is pointing toward. Whether that opposition comes from a stubborn family member, the needs of a newborn, or the hardships of war, I must think creatively and proactively about daily, weekly, monthly, seasonal, and annual habits that shape my life and enable me to perceive and receive God's invitations to beauty and its intertwined resistance.

I understand that without proper rest, exhaustion and burnout are unavoidable and will lead me away from restoration. Additionally, I will be unable to resist the patterns of the world—along with my own will, which often clashes with God's will. As a follower of Jesus, I'm called to work from a place of rest, not for it. In a performance-driven, productivity-focused culture, my body is harmed by the normalization of unsustainable habits. I do not desire to set a destructive example for others or orient my life around accumulation and achievement instead of delight, contemplation, and belovedness. I must work instead to receive my good Father's invitation to prioritize the sleep I need each night so I can be fully present to each day.

If I want to build a solid house and have the log of my life be knot free, rest each night is a solid foundation, but more is necessary. No matter the number of hours I sleep each night, my days are filled with opposition and opportunities to yield to the temptations of pride, narcissism, and hurry. Therefore, after I am well rested, I must discern which people, patterns, and practices truly replenish me—mentally, emotionally, physically, and spiritually.

Who are the people I need to see each week who love me well? What daily snacks or drinks genuinely bring me joy? What liturgies, sermons, or spiritual resources draw me into the presence of God? Figuring these things out is like gathering all of the materials to contribute to an environment that I can thrive in, with fruit to be enjoyed by those nearby and worldwide. Once I'm rested and restored, I am better equipped to resist, because the love of God and reality of his kingdom that I wish to receive and reflect will not go unopposed.

If I allow the Spirit of God to dwell in me, then I will have to confront the racism, prejudice, and White supremacy that tempt my own heart to compliance and those around me to complicity. I must continually contemplate my adoption into God's family and lovingly invite others to do the same. I must embrace the struggle to remain open and nondefensive in conversations about patriarchy and masculinity and reflect on the truth that I don't need to be perfect or play the messiah in every situation. I must sleep well and hold tightly to disciplines that orient me toward Jesus of Nazareth, not the false savior of White American Folk Religion, because if I end up choosing comfort and convenience to avoid confrontation and conflict, I will be in danger of having a dead faith (James 2:14-17) and no live relationship with Christ at all. My being and doing are intertwined, like my beauty and resistance.

And it is this conviction about beauty and resistance that stokes the curiosity of those around our family. Matthew 5:14-16 (NASB) says this:

> You are the light of the world. A city set on a hill cannot be hidden; nor do people light a lamp and put it under a basket, but on the lampstand, and it gives light to all who are in the house. Your light must shine before people in such a way that they may see your good works, and glorify your Father who is in heaven.

When someone asks, why do you sabbath? Have such a big party for Christmas? Take your kids to protest? Fight climate change? Resist political polarization? I must be ready, willing, and able—by God's grace and the Spirit's power—to point to the star around which I orient my words and deeds. From my times of individual and communal reflection will spring forth the good news of Jesus as Liberator, Savior, Messiah, and King. Out of rich times in prayer, Scripture, fasting, and worship individually and in community should come a testimony that edifies, encourages, and comforts those seeking to know more of and reflect Jesus in the world.

So what does setting up your own rhythms of rest, restoration, and resistance look like? In light of Lewin's force field and the five *I*'s of integrity (individual, intimate, interpersonal, institutional, ideology), we can fill in the chart shown in table 4.

Table 4. Uncovering rhythms of rest, restoration, and resistance

	Daily	Weekly	Monthly	Quarterly	Annually
Rest	When will you sleep and for how long? What can you do now to protect that time?	How can you take a 24-hour sabbath to stop and rest to create space for restoration?	What extended times of rest can you take once a month to center yourself on God and his will and work in the world?	What times can you set aside each season for rest and reflection that may be unavailable during another season?	Is there a time during the year that you can take a one- to two-week break from being productive and efficient?
Restore	What makes you feel fully alive? What connects you to God, yourself, and others? What can you do now to create, prepare for, and protect that time?	Who helps you feel loved and cared for? How often do you need to see them? What are some things you love to do that help you see and experience God, receive love, and feel happy?	Where are some places you can visit that are special and unique? What do you enjoy that you could share with those you love?	Consider the four seasons. What are some things you love to do that can only happen in fall, winter, spring, or summer that bring you joy?	Who are some people you could visit to help you feel loved, comforted, and encouraged? What places make you excited when you think about taking a trip there?
Resist	What individual, intimate, interpersonal, institutional, or ideological patterns of brokenness do you need to resist each day?	What habits and practices can you integrate into your sabbath to point to your life with God? What truths do you need to reflect on to ensure you take 24 hours off?	What habits and actions can you take to love your neighbors nearby and worldwide at least once a month? How much time and space can you set aside to learn about a justice issue, volunteer, or serve?	Do you need to reflect on how you spend your time, money, and energy to give and receive love? How can you use your time, money, and energy to better reflect your core values and beliefs?	What is a particular area of growth or change that you would like to spend extended work on? What events or initiatives take place each year that you may want to contribute to or participate in?

We can repeat our daily and weekly practices of rest and restoration in monthly, quarterly, and annual increments, which bring extraordinary benefits to both our individual and communal long-term health and fruitfulness. Rhythms like an annual two-week vacation or a quarterly overnight retreat give us the time and space to take a deeper inventory of what's happening in our lives—something a weekly sabbath or short reflection time often can't provide. These disciplines also help us create traditions with family and friends, wrapping our lives in intentionality and giving us meaningful benchmarks to look forward to.

For example, perhaps in the spring you go for a walk in the local botanical garden and in the fall you take a trip with friends to see the foliage or go apple picking. Then in the winter you lead a ministry dedicated to migrants and host a New Year's dinner for families from your local church. Income and accessibility can certainly be issues when considering how we can delight. Take note that sabbath and healthy rhythms that fill us up to be fruitful witnesses of our Lord Jesus do not have to be extravagant; they just need to be intentionally ours. My own rhythms are shown in table 5, with further elaboration below.

Table 5. My rhythms of rest, restoration, and resistance

	Daily	Weekly	Monthly	Quarterly	Annually
Rest	I need to sleep at least six hours per night. And I need to sleep before 12 a.m.	My sabbath is from Friday night to Saturday night. No emails, no chores.	One day per month I take an four- to eight-hour reflection time with God.	Four times per year, I need to go on a retreat, attend a conference, or meet with a mentor.	Take a two- or three-day trip alone to write, pray, and reflect. This can also include time visiting friends.
Restore	I need to move my body, listen to a podcast, and spend time in Scripture.\n\nI need to eat three solid meals and have my smoothie in the morning.	I need to spend meaningful time with Priscilla and the kids around good food and physical activity.\n\nPizza Fridays, smoothies with the kids, baking bread or brownies with them.	I need to connect with my brothers or friends who live far away.\n\nI need to get a massage or do a group sports activity.	In the summer it's time for barbecues and hosting. In the fall we enjoy the outdoors. In the winter, holidays and celebrations fill the schedule. And spring is full of birthday parties and outdoor trips.	A two-week vacation with family in a national park or somewhere naturally beautiful is a must.\n\nAlso, Priscilla and I take an annual trip to reconnect with one another without the kids.
Resist	Daily liturgy of the Lord's Prayer, Prayer of St. Francis, and Franciscan Benediction.\n\nPrayer of gratefulness and intercession for every meal.	Weekly scheduling with Priscilla and meal prep help us love one another well, steward our resources, and make time and space to honor our children and one another.	Every month we budget to ensure that our values are being reflected in how we spend our money.\n\nWe also attend a local dinner in our neighborhood where all are welcomed to have a meal.	We must celebrate and delight intentionally and orient ourselves around delight, justice, and contemplation. Not productivity and accumulation. Camping, Christmas, birthdays, and protests help us do that.	Once a year we lead or participate in a nonviolent protest.\n\nOnce a year we take a prolonged vacation away from technology and devices.

Rest. I operate most effectively when I've had between six and eight hours of sleep and go to bed before midnight. Weekly, I would like to take a sabbath that includes a good night's sleep along with no responses to emails. I need to keep my chores to a minimum and not run any errands. One day a month, I would like to take eight hours of silent retreat and reflection. In every season I would like to have an intentional meeting time with a mentor and a spiritual community that can edify, encourage, and challenge me. And annually, I would like to take a two- to three-day trip away from work and family on Labor Day weekend alone to be able to write, reflect, and see friends. I would also like to take at least a weeklong vacation that includes time in nature like a national park.

Restore. Every day I have to move my body, listen to a podcast, watch a video or show that stimulates my brain, and eat three solid meals, including my smoothie in the morning.[11] I also need to have meaningful connection with my wife and children, and that often comes through a game called Do You Really Know Your Family?[12] Weekly I need a sabbath that includes delicious food, physical activity, and meaningful time with Priscilla, my children, and Christian community. Every month, I need to connect with my brothers who do not live close by, and when I'm able to get a massage, it's rejuvenating. I also need to have times of celebration that orient me away from work and take creativity and imagination like birthdays, holidays, and family traditions.

Hosting and outdoor activities are what mark each season for me. In the summer it's restorative to take a one- or two-week vacation in a national park and visit local beaches with friends. In fall, an annual camping trip, hikes in Cold Spring, New York, and visiting trails upstate before it gets too cold have been wonderful practices. In winter, Christmas, New Year's, and Chinese New Year bring great joy because our home is full and loud with kids laughing, games, and deep conversations. In the spring, it's time to be outside again and celebrate birthdays. My youngest daughter, mother-in-law, and children's godfather all share the same birthday!

Finally, every year my wife and I take a two-week vacation that includes time with her extended family and extended quality time for just us and our children. We have also committed to an annual trip away from our children to sustain growth in our intimacy and connection.

Resist. Every day I pray prayers that press back against the deep insecurities I feel about my body and lovability, temptation toward comfort and accumulation, and anxiety about the future. The Lord's Prayer, the Prayer of Saint Francis, and the Franciscan Benediction are core to that. Moreover, I desire to cultivate gratefulness and contentment in my heart, be reminded of my dependence on God and others for provision, and center the least of these. So with every meal, I thank God and intercede for those who made my food possible and pray for those for whom a meal like this will need to come from God or neighbor.

Mealtime Prayer

Lord Jesus, thank you for this food. Would you bless it to our bodies and our bodies to your service. Be with those

who don't have food today, God, and those who made
this meal possible. Would they experience the same
community and provision that you've given us so
generously. Amen.

Every week, my wife and I plan for the week to come.
We plan for our sabbath, pursue times of connection with
one another, and make sure our kids will know they have
times to look forward to with us. We meal prep to minimize wasted food and the lure of eating out just to make
things easier. These efforts help us create space for one another, set expectations so we are kind and gracious toward
each other, and know what we have to offer our family and
neighbors who approach us with needs. It also helps us
be good stewards of the earth's resources by minimizing
plastic waste and other stresses on the environment that
come with eating takeout.

Every month my wife and I set our budget. We are confronted with how much money comes into our home and
goes toward our basic needs and the ways we've chosen
to delight and enjoy life. Budgeting for savings, tithing,
spending, and generosity pushes back against the constant
temptation toward comfort and convenience.

When our family chooses to orient our lives around rest,
delight, generosity, and celebration, we are modeling a different way of being for those who are closest to us. And
when I am asked why we do a certain tradition, I am able to
explain it with the five *I*'s in mind. For example, our annual

camping trip during Indigenous Peoples' weekend is a way for us to participate in remembrance of those whose land was taken while keeping family traditions.

Our times of vacation are an anchor in our year that let us disconnect from the pull to be productive, efficient, and economically and professionally significant. Our times of protest and nonviolent resistance remind us that things are not as they should be and we must contend for a world that is more just, loving, and kind. When we celebrate birthdays and anniversaries, we testify to the belovedness of each of us, our inherent worth, and our unmovable place in our family and community.

Without a rule of life or a set of disciplines to build on, we won't be able to stand against the patterns of our family, the world, or our personal preferences. We will fall apart. We need to establish rules of life that allow us to be rested and restored, enabling us to resist patterns of greed, pride, and oppression while reflecting the kingdom of God. By doing so, we can repeat those redemptive patterns and actions in the world. Discipline is necessary for us to respond as sons and daughters of the Most High God rather than react out of obligation, fear, or the need to appear productive.

Whatever we commit to, we must debrief and reflect so we know the seeds we are planting bear the fruit we are looking for. Table 6 contains some questions you can ask before you begin and when you are taking inventory:

Table 6. The four *R*'s

	Prepare	Debrief
Rest	**Go to sleep.** When will you sleep? What can you do now to protect that time?	**How are you sleeping?** 0 (awful) to 5 (amazing) Why? What needs to change to make next week/month a 5?
Restore	What makes you feel fully alive? What connects you to God, yourself, and others? What can you do now to prepare for and protect that time?	What did you do? How did you experience restoration? 0 (awful) to 5 (amazing) Why? What needs to change to make next week/month a 5?
Resist	What personal, relational, and systemic patterns of brokenness do you need to resist this week? What can you do now and what help do you need to prepare to resist this week?	What conscious choices did you make this week/month to join God in the renewal of all things? What fruit did you observe (external and internal)? How did you define success? What if anything would you change?
Repeat	As a result of practicing the four *R*'s this week/month, what are you beginning to realize?	In light of what you are realizing, what do you feel and think?

FALLING SHORT, MAKING CHANGES

When you establish a rule of life and it takes root, it can be tempting to hold fast to it and resist change. This is especially true if your family and community are taking part and you experience fruitfulness from it. We strongly desire to be finished and check off an accomplishment. Sadly, this is not how the kingdom of God works. To follow Jesus is to embrace the reality that his kingdom has come and simultaneously is coming.

We must be like Jesus and resist being like the Pharisees when they confronted him for allowing his disciples to pick and eat grain on the Sabbath (Mark 2:23-28). Jesus proclaimed that the Sabbath was made to meet the needs of people and not people to meet the requirements of the Sabbath. Shortly after, the Pharisees again challenged Jesus when he healed a man with a withered hand on the Sabbath (Mark 3:1-6).

What the Pharisees and religious leaders of the day failed to recognize was that because of their commitment to rituals designed to bring them closer to God, they were missing God in their midst. I am often guilty of the same ignorance. I can embrace the disciplines and appreciate how they make me feel so strongly that I forget their original purpose. The story I told myself was that the scaffolding of my post-sabbatical life was leading to fruitfulness that extended beyond myself and my family into my community. I truly enjoyed what had I built. What I failed to realize, just like the Pharisees, was that change was on the horizon. God was doing something different, and because of my spiritual disciplines, I was missing him.

When Jesus shows up, I have several choices in how I respond. Option one is that I behave like the Pharisees, resist change, and dismiss the call of Jesus because I like the way things are. The fruit of this would be self-righteousness and the construction of an elaborate false self held together for my own comfort and stability. This is something I am already aware of and don't want to do.

Option two is that I just give up because change is difficult and I'm unsure if I can trust that these new habits and patterns will be as fruitful as what I had before. The fruit of this would be a musty spirituality that sits idle as time passes, revisited only when I remember what could have been while not working toward what could be. This is tempting for me because it is self-centered, allowing me to shirk responsibility over my discipleship and shift the blame onto someone or something else.

Last is option three, where I begin to build a new scaffolding and embrace the reality that the work of God on this side of heaven is always a work in progress. This is the hardest but certainly the right choice.

A few years ago I was at church when someone asked if I had a social life. My wife laughed, because the answer was clearly that I did not. I was ashamed. Shortly after Covid started, we moved from one neighborhood to another, changed churches, and had a child less than two years old who needed constant attention. The story I told myself was that I needed to do everything. I told myself I couldn't ask my wife for help because she was so tired from work as a professional educator leading in the midst of a generational crisis. I told myself that reaching out to people to hang out would be too inconvenient and too much work. I believed I was doing the virtuous thing by working my fingers to the bone for my family.

This was my genogram and counter-formation rising to the surface. I needed to take some steps toward reorienting myself, because there were ideological, interpersonal, and intimate knots in the trunk of my life that pushed patterns of rest and restoration to the side. It is certainly true that parenting small children is demanding and that season can be very intense. But I could have had support if I had allowed myself to ask for it.

I was praying my prayers, listening to my podcasts, and caught up on my shows. But I wasn't taking care of myself through play, delight, or fellowship. I rarely conversed with peers in casual conversation. My adult interactions were dominated by purpose and productivity, and I told myself they had to be. Taking care of two kids, cooking meals, keeping things clean, and more were all *my* responsibility. I was in a spin cycle and unable to get out. I was married to a ritual because I liked the rhythm. But it was time for new scaffolding because my conditions had changed.

So when the opportunity for a nine-month discipleship course at church came up, my wife signed me up! I got to go through a rich cohort experience studying Rich Villodas's book *The Deeply Formed Life* that culminated in an overnight retreat.

Was it perfect? No! Because no book, program, or project is. And that is the wrong question anyway. This course broke me out of the cycle and exposed the sin of pride in my heart. When I told someone I was taking the course, they asked, "Couldn't you teach this?" And the answer was yes. There were certainly elements I could have contributed to. But the question was *should* I teach it. And the answer was a resounding no. I firmly believe that if I am pouring out,

I should be poured into, and I need to sit down for three hours every two weeks to get to know people who want to get to know me as a person. Not as a leader, preacher, teacher, or facilitator—just me. I needed to learn that. Sarah and Jose, who were part of the cohort, leaned in, listened, and loved me, and I was able to lean in, listen, and learn from them.

It was healing to be with them. I didn't learn anything revolutionary, but I did a revolutionary thing for my soul. I was reoriented to my life as it is—not how I feared it would be. I am a human being, not a human doing. My kids would be okay if I went out for a few hours; the house would still get cleaned, and food would be on the table. If I took care of myself, Jesus would take care of everything else, and he would show me where he needed me to show up. Jesus, not Jonathan, actually held my life together. Christ had supremacy (Colossians 1:15-20), not me. Hallelujah and amen.

Cultivating openness to beauty and resistance requires time, space, and intentionality. Over time, understanding what sparks joy and fills us, along with knowing what takes true effort and leaves us drained, helps us engage for the long term and prioritize our being alongside our doing. Equally important is to embrace the theological truth that scaffolding will always be either going up or coming down, making way for new growth. Creation is being made new, and so are we. The scaffolding is evidence that God is working, holding us together, and renewing us as well.

It is through our willingness to confess, repent, and be reconciled to God that we can become ministers of reconciliation. Our qualification for God's work stems from our willingness to be shaped and transformed by God. And it is out of that transformation that we join God in the renewal of all things to reflect the beauty of his kingdom and resist the patterns of this world.

RECUPERATE

why can't i just get started?

When I turned thirty years old, I had four surgeries on my feet. While playing paintball during a workplace retreat, I struck the side of my foot on a rock. It hurt, but I thought it was a bruise. After three weeks of pain that did not subside, I decided to go to the doctor. I remember going into the sterile environment committed to telling the truth in this new decade of my life. After all, my foot really hurt and I had health insurance, so there was no need to "man up" or hide anything.

When the doctor asked for an x-ray, I thought that was normal, but when he put the images on the screen, I realized my foot wasn't. There was a fracture on the outside of my foot where fluid had begun to collect. Not only that, I had a bone spur in my ankle, ligament damage in my foot, and a bunion at the base of my big toe.

Upon seeing all of this and noticing I had fallen arches, the doctor asked to examine my other foot. That x-ray showed similar damage. The bone spur in that ankle was larger and the ligament damage more severe. There was also a bone spur on the outside of my pinky toe and a bunion on the big toe. He told me all of this in one go while pointing to the problem spots, unfazed by the information he was sharing.

I thought to myself, *No wonder my feet hurt.*

A little stunned, I asked the doctor what he recommended we do. He said I would need two days of surgery spread out over five months. First they would do my right foot. He would take the bunion from my big toe and use the bone fragments to fill the fracture on the outside of the foot. He seemed excited that I had some extra bone he could use to fix my foot, like a chef who realized he had extra sausage for another recipe.

He would then repair my ligaments and shave down the bone spur in my ankle. After that healed, he would work on my left foot. My ankle would be repaired, bone spur and bunion shaved. I nodded like I knew what that meant and asked if it could be scheduled in a way that would max out my deductible.

He said, "Of course," then asked about my history with sports. I shared about the separated shoulder from touch football a decade earlier that didn't get repaired, the many times I toughed it out after a twist or a sprain. Then I went deeper.

I admitted I didn't have the greatest coaches, and my school district didn't have the best resources. When I got hurt, they just taped it up and asked, "Can you go?" I knew what it meant to say no. I would become insignificant, relegated to ride the pine for the rest of the season. I would be one of those kids who came with the team but didn't play, and I never wanted to be a spectator again. Injured players were discarded, and I did not want to be thrown away like a defective toy. So I would get on that football or soccer field until I had to be carried off. That's what it meant to be a man, right? That's what it meant to be good. All the legends did this, right?

As I was sharing this with the doctor, I thought about my wife's responses when I had told her about my various soccer and football injuries over the years. "They didn't take care of you," she would say. But I would dismiss her and defend them. I didn't know what else to do.

I can see now that I was avoiding my anger, defending people I identified with so I wouldn't be seen as backward, under-resourced, poor, desperate, or stupid. That's how I felt in that doctor's office in Manhattan. I felt uncared for, desperate, stupid, and poor. My unprocessed feelings had determined reality for me. Now I was s dealing with the consequences.

The truth is that when I was a kid, there was one doctor two towns over, and we didn't have health insurance. I don't remember seeing an orthopedist for any of my injuries. And I definitely did not get a second opinion on anything. There was one option and what that doctor said was it. Brodnax and Manhattan were completely different worlds, and I didn't have to defend life in either one. But I did have to live in reality in both of them, which seemed more difficult than hobbling around with creaky joints.

The doctor assured me he would fix me up and I would be back to whatever sport I wanted to play—as long as I went to physical therapy. He said his surgery days were Fridays and that I'd need someone to get me home after the anesthesia.

A month later I was in surgery, and the doctor, staff, and propofol all did their jobs. My foot was huge and I was delirious leaving the surgical center. I provided some quality entertainment for my good friend Courtney, who got me back home. My first daughter was just six months old, so friends came by to vacuum, take out the trash, and do our laundry. They delivered food and held our eldest daughter so her mom could sleep.

Then I had to go to follow-up appointments and physical therapy, which revealed more problems. Walking for so long on flat feet with unaddressed knee and ankle problems affected my back and hips. The lower half of my body was a symphony of instruments playing in the wrong key, but the physical therapist assured me that if I kept coming, I would recover. And they were right. After five months I felt pretty good. Then it was time to do it all over again on my left foot. Assessment, surgery, funny ride home, friends helping, and more physical therapy. A year and a half later, I was wearing the right shoes, along with braces and orthotics. Only then could I begin a new workout regimen.

THE FAST WORDS REAL SLOW

Often in drug commercials, pharmaceutical companies will recite side effects and potential dangers at hyperspeed after you've been reeled in by the promise of the product.

Sometimes these warnings include innocuous effects like headache or back pain, whereas at other times the conditions are more serious and occur in one-third of cases. I want you to know that after reading and engaging with this content and experiencing a potential desire to jump in, you may not be ready. The first step for you might be recuperation.

Recuperation after an injury refers to the process of recovering health, strength, and function after physical harm. This involves a period of rest, healing, and rehabilitation that allows the body to repair damaged tissues, regain mobility, and recover strength. The specific steps and duration depend on the severity and type of injury, but it typically includes stopping the activity that caused the damage to allow time to address the injury. Rest allows the body to heal by avoiding activities that may worsen the damage. Next is rehabilitation as you gradually introduce normal actions and habits in a way that prevents further damage as you move toward full strength.

Often during the process you must manage pain with things like medication, ice, heat, and stretching. Follow-up care with doctors and specialists helps you know if your recovery is going well or the plan needs adjustment. The goal of recuperation is to achieve full recovery and prevent future damage. I name all of these steps because before I could implement a rule of life for beauty and resistance, I had to heal from the harm caused by lack of boundaries, a broken genogram, and systemic injustice.

Relentless effort is not what we were made for. It profoundly misshapes us and does violence to our souls. My unaddressed damage prevents me from making long-term change. Most of us are walking around with wounds that have not been acknowledged or treated. *Forbes* reports that 80 percent of people in the United States have experienced emotional abuse and 75 percent say their boss is the most stressful part of the day.[1] Moreover, 25 percent of men and nearly 50 percent of women have experienced some sort of abusive behavior from an intimate partner.[2] This means the vast majority of the people we encounter each day are carrying trauma and all people are connected to someone who has experienced abuse in some way. There have been days, months, or years when many people have heard more cursing than blessings, more insults than encouragement, and seen more violence than they want to remember.

This is not the soil for a significant life change, new workout regimen, or commitment to an expensive conference or retreat. This is soil in need of regeneration and time to lie fallow so it may be fruitful again.

MISSHAPEN MENTALITY

We live in an oppressed world. All of us. Every person of color and all those racially assigned White. Menfolk, womenfolk, and nonbinary folk. Those who are rich, poor, educated, uneducated, married, partnered, single, and divorced. The stranger, the immigrant, the undocumented, and the citizen.

The teenager, parent, infant, and widowed. Every single person you see, meet, tweet at, or text is oppressed by forces both supernatural and manmade. To deny that about yourself or others is to deny reality.

Ephesians 6:10-12 and 1 Peter 5:8 highlight the spiritual battle humanity finds itself locked in from the moment we are born. The resistance to our individual and communal flourishing is unrelenting via coloniality, White American Folk Religion, and its willful participants and protectors.

Every day, while we are attempting to resist the evil one and his schemes, we are kept in the boxes made for us by powers and principalities and people faithful to them. We are like square watermelons or tiny bonsai trees. *Bonsai* literally means "grown in a container," and these naturally large trees are forced to stay small.[3] Similarly, to get square watermelons you start with healthy plants and place them in a square container. Once ripened, the fruits are picked and fit nicely into refrigerators and other storage boxes.[4]

Our container is society, and it is around us at all times. Though it looks like we are growing, we are surviving on the most basic nutrients available to us, cut off from community, and forced to develop against our created nature, but we are pleasing to those who hold the keys to the glass boxes we are in. There seems to be no option to disengage or escape. There is only participation through complicity, complacency, or coercion.

This terrible process of de-formation happens to the powerful and the powerless of every background, heritage, and income bracket. Native New Yorker, Brooklyn-based writer, and novelist Robert Jones Jr. has written the most amazing and awful passages I have ever read about the reality of oppression. His prose is amazing because of its pace, word choice, and power. It is awful because it's true.

The Prophets mixes poetry and prose and sounds like a written recording of how Black people talk set to an internal music that readers of all backgrounds are invited to listen to. In the following citation, Isaiah and Samuel are two enslaved men on a plantation who think deeply and wrestle constantly with the impact of enslavement on themselves and the community. Ultimately, Isaiah chooses to run away and Samuel chooses to stay.

"I get tired. But I want to live," [Isaiah] said.

See, that was where Isaiah had faltered. To survive in this place, you had to want to die. That was the way of the world as remade by toubab [an African word for someone of European descent], and Samuel's list of grievances was long. They pushed people into the mud and then called them filthy. They forbade people from accessing any knowledge of the world and then called them simple. They worked people until their empty hands were twisted, bleeding, and could do no more, then called them lazy. They forced people to eat innards from troughs and then called them uncivilized. They kidnapped babies and shattered families and then called them incapable of love. They raped and lynched and cut up people into parts and called the pieces savages. They stepped on people's throats with all their might and asked why the people couldn't breathe. And then, when people made an attempt to break the foot, or cut it off one, they screamed "CHAOS!" and claimed that mass murder was the only way to restore order.

They praised every daisy and then called every black-berry a stain. They bled the color from God's face, gave it a dangle between its legs, and called it holy. Then, when they were done breaking things, they pointed at the sky and called the color of the universe itself a sin. And the whole world believed them, even some of Samuel's people. Especially some of Samuel's people. This was untoward and made it hard to open your heart, to feel a sense of loyalty that wasn't a strategy. It was easier to just seal yourself up and rock yourself to sleep.[5]

Isaiah saw his conditions and knew in his bones that despite all that was aligned against him, life on a plantation was no way for a human being to live. In fact, enslavement, colonization, domination, and constant hiding to remain unwhipped was no life at all. Enslavers believed the lie that they were superior, and some of those who were enslaved believed it too. But Isaiah's relationship with Samuel showed him that something new, different, and liberating was possible. Once he believed that, it was like warm light to a moth in the darkness; he had to run toward it.

I suspect that many of us want to run but are so injured that we need time and community to get us ready to look up, stand, wobble, walk, shuffle, then sprint. We need emotional scaffolding.

EMOTIONAL SCAFFOLDING

In education, emotional scaffolding is a supportive framework that a teacher, parent, partner, or friend provides to help a student navigate emotional challenges, develop emotional regulation, and build resilience.[6] This involves offering empathy, encouragement, and guidance in moments of emotional distress while allowing the individual to gradually take more responsibility for managing their emotions over time. The goal is to create a safe environment for emotional growth, ensuring the student feels understood and supported but also empowered to handle their emotions independently as they mature.[7]

This emotional scaffolding might include validation, modeling appropriate emotional responses, and teaching coping strategies, all while adjusting the level of support as the person's emotional skills develop. In an ideal world, parents, siblings, grandparents, aunts, uncles, and the proverbial village give the necessary support structures for a child to flourish interdependently. Churches, sports teams, coaches, mentors, and colleagues are all integral figures who can create the conditions necessary to hold someone up and together amid change, difficulty, and growth.

Sadly, we do not live in this ideal world, and because of that, the emotional scaffolding necessary for children to build solid emotional lives is often not there. I think with sadness of the many collapses in my own childhood when my tiny heart and mind were trying to build a coherent emotional life. I feel even more sadness when I think of my own imperfections and the potential collapses of my own kids' emotions. My wife's therapist told her once that much of our formation happens before we even speak. Often we spend twenty years in therapy trying to undo what we learned in the first three years of life.

I have a friend who researched the effects of racism on kids. She shared with me that children in preschool understand how racism works, particularly anti-Blackness. A primal need for emotional safety and the clear, present danger of White supremacy closed in on me as a Black child without the resources—either tangible or intangible—to process the world in all its wonder, worries, and wars. This explains much of my longing.

My early awareness of White supremacy and anti-Blackness, along with a lack of emotional scaffolding, left me in an emotional desert. What I truly needed was an emotional ecosystem where love, acceptance, and belonging were constant. It took many years, but eventually my sabbatical gave me space, and my professional and relational network provided connections to receive some of the emotional scaffolding I had lacked in my early years of life.

I shared this in group therapy, and one person remarked again that it takes a lifetime to undo what people do to us early in life. Realizing this, I am now learning how to give and receive love without strategy or fear (1 John 4:18). I choose to walk in that frightening truth because Jesus' perfect love drives out fear. Just as Isaiah tasted freedom and craved more, I have experienced the love, acceptance, and belonging I've always sought and was made for. Without the conscious choice to recuperate after burning out, I would not have experienced this reality.

After being in this professional setting of therapy and support, I realized my mother had her "group" with her siblings and coworkers. She couldn't afford a sabbatical, but she made space regularly to get the care and comfort she needed while offering it too. Every Sunday night my aunt would call and they would share updates, parenting advice, and simple presence with one another. During times when my mom and dad were having a particularly rough season, she and her teacher's aide would commute together to process the conflict before she came back home. Looking back, I can see that my mom didn't need a crowd but a few people who were consistent. And she had that. Now it was my turn to figure out how to do the same.

JESUS SAID, "IT IS FINISHED"

I must choose to recuperate when needed, because if I fall and can't get up, Jesus doesn't put me on the bench. He pulls me aside because he loves me, and being with me matters more to him than anything I could do for him. After all, he said, "It is finished" on the cross, so what more is there for me to do?

I must hold fast to this reality because, as Robert Jones Jr. so eloquently said, if we are pushed into the mud and called lazy, cut into pieces and called savage, and forced to eat slop from troughs and called uncivilized—an indictment that has been over my family and heritage for generations—it feels inescapable. There is much work needed to fully reclaim my humanity. And what about all of us becoming truly human together? It seems impossible—unless there is a Savior who can destroy the hierarchy, redefining value and worth as thoroughly as the colonizer once imposed it.

To drink from that wellspring of life when one has been parched for so long may take more than the same prayers twice a day, a sabbath once a week, and an overnight retreat once a year. The woundedness you might hold could need intensive care that includes therapy, stepping down from the position you hold, or backing off from some responsibilities on your plate. Not because you can't do them or you're not good enough, but because you don't have to prove your value and worth.

Recuperation is an invitation to slowly ground yourself in beauty and resistance, to explore wonder as a goal in itself.

That's what watching Pixar flicks, listening to jazz, and getting really good at baking gooey brownies was for me. When the season changed, I could take stock of where I was, change my rule of life, or recuperate again because I am accepted and God is not ashamed of me. I am his and he is mine. I'm a child of the Most High God.

Perhaps you realize you're in a prolonged season of burnout or need to leave a toxic faith community. Maybe you've left an abusive relationship or workplace and need time to heal, explore, and recenter. Maybe you were pricked in the best way by a good sermon. Or perhaps you've noticed complacency in your heart and mind and long for a deeper connection with God and others. Whatever the case, following Jesus starts by cultivating a relationship with him. Prioritizing that in your rule of life means being open to change as new challenges or opportunities arise—whether it's the birth of a child, the loss of a loved one, or conflicts and turmoil that come your way.

A solid place to start is to choose one rhythm to keep you grounded and one person to carry you through. Perhaps you need to find a counselor or therapist and meet with them every two weeks. Maybe you need to call a friend and let them know you're willing to cook breakfast, take them to lunch, or buy a coffee if you can spend time together every two weeks. Or it might be time for you to find a local AA or other twelve-step program and find your people and rhythm there. Whatever you do, it doesn't have to be big, extravagant, or expensive. It just needs to be intentional, accessible, and yours.

Two relationships that have been pivotal for me after my sabbatical have been one-on-one meetings with a coach and having a small huddle of people pray for me once a month. I need to talk with someone every week about how I'm doing in my marriage and inner life so I get used to sharing my feelings, because it's easy for me to perform or hide. And now that my mom is gone, I need to know there are people praying for me. These two rituals have been key planks and pipes holding me up and together this season.

With all of our flaws and shortcomings, I believe in my core that God created us with a desire for personal and social renewal and shalom. This is not a revolutionary idea, but to live out this reality requires a revolution of values and practices that pushes back against all that entices us away from the straight and narrow path to receive the abundance God has for us.

Christ and the great cloud of witnesses testify to the truth that humanity was made out of love for love, justice, and shalom—peace between all relationships. If we take up our cross and follow Jesus, we will share in the resurrection and life abundant on this side of heaven and the next. I am convinced that life on this side of glory is full of beauty and resistance. And we must posture ourselves to receive both in ever-increasing measure as our good Father makes them ever available to us, his kids.

EPILOGUE

CHANGE OF PLANS

I am standing on the threshold of who I want to be
looking back at who I am
and wondering why I didn't see this before.

They say that hindsight is 20/20
then my foresight must have been like 50/100
and my insight like a blind man fondling the darkness
for a light switch in a room with no walls.

Because when I took this path I thought I was taking
  route progress.
I assumed I was going down the road that was the best
by taking the track more traveled but instead
I jumped on train lack of self-respect,
ended up depressed, distressed, and signaling SOS to
  strangers in all directions.

I don't want to be another doctor, another lawyer, or
    bite my nails in an office.
I want to heal heart wounds with my words,
prosecute politicians with my pen, and
invest in audiences willing to listen to a
    Columbia graduate
who wanted so bad to drop out but couldn't because
my Momma taught me the value of an education.

So I'm changing my major from biology pre-med to
    major in life
with a double concentration in success and excellence.
My courses include three semesters of charity,
two on goodwill towards man
and a required seminar on increasing my measure
    of faith.

My thesis proves man must know his past
before he understands his present
or comprehends his future and I live out my
    Savior's motto
that to whom much is given,
so much more is required.

I don't see life like it is.
I close my eyes and envision how it could be
and then slave to make my dreams a reality.

I hope you love me for trying to make this world a
    better place
for the next generation and I promise your hard-
    earned money is not going to waste.

My words are all I have so I hope you take them and
    save them in that special
place that the world's expectations can't get to.

I met God and now I have to live like I know who he is.

I wrote this poem in 2006 shortly after I heard God's
audible voice for the first time telling me to leave my job as
a real estate agent and trust him to provide for me. Because
people wanted to see prospective homes when they were off
work, I was working on the weekends running open houses.
I wasn't going to church or seeing my friends much. I was
trying to find myself in a city that had no shortage of sug-
gestions for who I should be.

One snowy Sunday morning, I thought surely my boss
would give me the day off and I would not be required
to show a home. I was wrong. So there I was at the office
printing off sign-in sheets and stuffing photos in the
folders. My boss called my phone and sounded frustrated
about something. He raised his voice and I raised mine.
The call ended and I don't remember what was said. I only
remember asking out loud, "Why do I feel like I don't
belong here?"

A voice answered, "Because you don't."

There was no one else in that building on Seventeenth and Sixth Avenue that cold January morning. So I put in my two weeks' notice that day. I didn't have a plan, but I had a word from the Lord, and that's all I needed that day. I hope this book was a word for you and you have a bit of what you need to do the next right thing. You are loved deeply by God and he desires to make all things new, including you and every piece of creation you see around you. You are not a passive observer but an active participant receiving and reflecting the kingdom of God.

Jesus will hold you up and together as you seek beauty and resistance and see his word go forth and not return empty, accomplishing the purposes for which it was sent (Isaiah 55:11). He will send his Spirit to fill and guide you and people to journey with you on this side of heaven. And I trust that the same God who shook the prison that held Paul and Silas, sent an angel to Elizabeth to herald John the Baptist, and did not spare his only begotten Son calls you his beloved and will provide for your needs.

ACKNOWLEDGMENTS

My name is the only one on the cover of this book, but I am not the only one responsible for the words that fill these pages. I am deeply grateful to my wife, Priscilla, who shows me daily what it looks like to live out our vows amid much wonder and difficulty. There is no Sayulita, no title, no stories, no book without her. I am also grateful for my daughters, Maia and Everest, who show me what it looks like to play, be present, and learn to love and be loved in ways I didn't know I could. I want to express sincere gratitude to Ashley Hong from Gardner Literary Agency who went above and beyond what I expected and Al Hsu and everyone at InterVarsity Press for another amazing experience. It is a privilege to serve the ministry that served me so many years ago. I also want to thank my intercessors, therapists, counselors, and close friends named and unnamed throughout the book who modeled faithful wrestling and prodded me closer to Jesus. And finally, thank you to all of the cohort participants, alumni, and subscribers who joined calls, met up in person, and shared your lives with me. It was all of you who taught me that beauty is just as important as resistance, and the best resistance is full of beauty. God is faithful and your support and partnership is evidence of that abundant truth.

To him who is able to keep you from stumbling and to present you before his glorious presence without fault and with great joy—to the only God our Savior be glory, majesty, power and authority, through Jesus Christ our Lord, before all ages, now and forevermore! Amen. (Jude 24-25)

NOTES

1. THE RECKONING

1 James Madison University, *Racial Terror: Lynching in Virginia*, accessed January 7, 2025, https://sites.lib.jmu.edu/valynchings; U.S. History Scene, "Excerpts from the Virginia Black Codes (1866)," accessed January 7, 2025, https://ushistory scene.com/article/excerpts-virginia-black-codes-1866.

2 Jami Snead, "Highlighting Mecklenburg's Black Schools: East End High School," *The News Progress*, February 4, 2021, www.thenewsprogress.com/community /article_10a2a360-66f5-11eb-a902-e3359697bc67.html.

3 Gloria Oladipo, "US Police Killed Record Number of People in 2022," *The Guardian*, January 6, 2023, www.theguardian.com/us-news/2023/jan/06/us-police -killings-record-number-2022.

4 Adam Serwer, "The Cruelty Is the Point," *The Atlantic*, October 4, 2018, www .theatlantic.com/ideas/archive/2018/10/the-cruelty-is-the-point/572104.

5 Associated Press, "Trump Mocks Ford's Claims Against Kavanaugh," YouTube, October 3, 2018, 1 min., 37 sec., www.youtube.com/watch?v=2m00qAeFHaQ.

6 David A. Graham, "Trump to Police: 'Please Don't Be Too Nice' to Suspects," ABC News, July 28, 2017, https://abcnews.go.com/Politics/trump-police-nice-suspects /story?id=48914504; CNN, "Trump Mocks Reporter with Disability," YouTube, November 25, 2015, 45 sec., www.youtube.com/watch?v=PX9reO3QnUA.

7 Laura Kurtzman, "Trump's 'Chinese Virus' Tweet Linked to Rise in Anti-Asian Hashtags on Twitter," University of California San Francisco, March 19, 2021, www.ucsf.edu/news/2021/03/420081/trumps-chinese-virus-tweet-linked -rise-anti-asian-hashtags-twitter.

8 Rebecca Santana and Elliot Spagat, "Settlement over Trump-Era Family Separations at the Border Limits Future Separations for 8 Years," PBS NewsHour, December 16, 2024, www.pbs.org/newshour/politics/settlement-over-trump-era -family-separations-at-the-border-limits-future-separations-for-8-years; Daniel Bush, "Trump's Decision to End DACA, Explained," PBS NewsHour, September 5, 2017, www.pbs.org/newshour/nation/trumps-decision-end-daca-explained; Jeffrey Cohen, "The Racial Demagoguery of Trump's Assaults on Colin Kaepernick

and Steph Curry," *The New Yorker*, September 25, 2017, www.newyorker.com /news/daily-comment/the-racial-demagoguery-of-trumps-assaults-on-colin -kaepernick-and-steph-curry.

[9] Courtney Vinopal, "What We Know About the Atlanta Spa Shootings that Killed 8, Including 6 Asian Women," PBS NewsHour, March 18, 2021, www.pbs.org /newshour/nation/what-we-know-about-the-atlanta-spa-shootings-that-killed -8-including-6-asian-women.

2. REST

[1] Mindsoother Therapy Center, "Infinity Loop: Identifying Negative Cycles in Your Relationship," *Mindsoother Blog*, March 8, 2022, www.mindsoother.com/blog /infinity-loop-identifying-negative-cycles-in-your-relationship.

[2] M. Robert Mulholland Jr., "The Deeper Journey: The False Self vs. the Christ Self," Transforming Center, last modified July 2016, https://transformingcenter.org /2016/07/deeper-journey-false-self-christ-self.

[3] Dana Roc, "Poet, Activist, and Speaker, Jonathan Walton," http://danaroc.com /inspiring_073012jonathanwalton.html.

[4] Roc, "Jonathan Walton."

[5] Mulholland, "The Deeper Journey."

[6] Jonathan P. Walton, *Twelve Lies That Hold America Captive* (Downers Grove, IL: InterVarsity Press, 2019); Jonathan P. Walton, *The Emotionally Health Activist Course* (independently published, 2022).

[7] Daniel Silliman and Kate Shellnutt, "Ravi Zacharias Hid Hundreds of Pictures of Women, Abuse During Massages, and a Rape Allegation," *Christianity Today*, February 11, 2021, www.christianitytoday.com/2021/02/ravi-zacharias -rzim-investigation-sexual-abuse-sexting-rape.

[8] Mike Cosper, *The Rise and Fall of Mars Hill* (podcast), Christianity Today, originally released June 21, 2021, to November 10, 2022, www.christianitytoday.com /podcasts/the-rise-and-fall-of-mars-hill; Bob Allen, "John Piper Blames Abuse of Women on 'Egalitarian Myth,'" Baptist News Global, March 20, 2018, https://baptist news.com/article/john-piper-blames-abuse-of-women-on-egalitarian-myth.

[9] Munther Isaac, "The War in Gaza: A Palestinian Pastor/Theologian's Perspective," *Theology in the Raw* (podcast), released November 2023, https://theologyintheraw .com/podcast/the-war-in-gaza-a-palestinian-pastor-theologians-perspective-dr -rev-munther-isaac.

[10] Carter G. Woodson, *The Mis-education of the Negro* (Washington, DC: Associated Publishers, 1933), 84.

[11] Victor Lebow, "Price Competition in 1955," *Journal of Retailing* 31, no. 1 (Spring 1955): 5-10, 42, 44.

[12] Louise Story, "Anywhere the Eye Can See, It's Likely to See an Ad," *The New York Times*, January 15, 2007, www.nytimes.com/2007/01/15/business/media /15everywhere.html.

[13] Laura Ceci, "Average Time Spent per Day on Smartphone in the United States 2021," Statista, June 14, 2022, www.statista.com/statistics/1224510/time-spent-per-day-on-smartphone-us.

[14] Bill Hathaway, "Stress Makes Life's Clock Tick Faster—Chilling Out Slows It Down," *Yale News*, December 6, 2021, https://news.yale.edu/2021/12/06/stress-makes-lifes-clock-tick-faster-chilling-out-slows-it-down.

[15] Agnese Mariotti, "The Effects of Chronic Stress on Health: New Insights into the Molecular Mechanisms of Brain-Body Communication," *Future Science OA* 1, no. 3 (Nov 1, 2015): FSO23, https://doi.org/10.4155/fso.15.21.

[16] Thomas Merton, *Conjectures of a Guilty Bystander* (New York: Doubleday, 1966), 73.

[17] Tricia Hersey, *Rest Is Resistance: A Manifesto* (New York: Little, Brown Spark, 2022).

[18] Alison Burke, "Working-Class White Americans Are Now Dying in Middle Age at Faster Rates Than Minority Groups," Brookings, March 23, 2017, www.brookings.edu/articles/working-class-white-americans-are-now-dying-in-middle-age-at-faster-rates-than-minority-groups.

[19] Josh Bivens and Jori Kandra, "CEO Pay Has Skyrocketed 1,460% Since 1978," Economic Policy Institute, October 4, 2022, www.epi.org/publication/ceo-pay-in-2021.

[20] "History of Federal Minimum Wage Rates Under the Fair Labor Standards Act, 1938-2009," US Department of Labor, accessed February 18, 2025, www.dol.gov/agencies/whd/minimum-wage/history/chart.

[21] Bernice Johnson Reagon, "Sweet Honey in the Rock: Come Unto Me (Raise Your Voice)," YouTube, posted by Amado McCarroll-Gallegos, December 31, 2018, 2 min., 44 sec., www.youtube.com/watch?v=lLN3rs1KYgI&list=PLeb9zWBI65_mAtApy4lacFceOhUCx3W5l&index=21.

3. RESTORE

[1] French Workshop in Bayside, Queens, is where I encountered Earl Grey in all its glory in this almond-flour-based cookie. It is a temptation on every trip to and from our home.

[2] "Fact Sheet: Single-Use Plastics," EarthDay.org, March 29, 2022, www.earthday.org/fact-sheet-single-use-plastics.

[3] Te Rautini "Peace/Afio Mai," YouTube, posted by Te Rautini, December 8, 2019, 9 min., 16 sec., www.youtube.com/watch?v=jyFnP6iRKg8.

[4] Moya Bailey, a Black feminist scholar, created the term *misogynoir* in 2010 to address the ways in which Black women are marginalized in both mainstream and Black communities. Misogynoir, the oppressive intersection of anti-Blackness and misogyny, can manifest as negative portrayals of Black women, the hypersexualization of Black women's bodies, and the devaluation of their voices and experiences. See Moya Bailey, *Misogynoir Transformed: Black Women's Digital Resistance* (New York: NYU Press, 2021).

[5] Clifford Krauss, "Russian Bomber, Once in U.S. Airspace, Returns to Russia," CNN, February 11, 2008, www.cnn.com/2008/US/02/11/russian.bomber, archived March 3, 2008 at https://web.archive.org/web/20080305030151/http://www.cnn.com/2008/US/02/11/russian.bomber/.

[6] Christina Zhao, "Cops Shut Down 'White Lives Matter' Rally in Huntington Beach That Turned Violent After 90 Minutes," *Newsweek*, April 11, 2021, www.newsweek.com/cops-shut-down-white-lives-matter-rally-huntington-beach-that-turned-violent-90-minutes-1582751.

[7] Code-switching is what occurs when people of one race, class, status, or other social classification alternate between two or more languages, dialects, or communication styles within a conversation or social interaction, depending on the context or audience. People often code-switch to fit into different social, cultural, or professional environments, adapting their speech or behavior to meet the expectations of that group. This is especially true for racialized groups in the United States who change their accents and word choices to appear good, safe, and acceptable to those in power, authority, or influence.

4. RESIST

[1] Graham Bensinger, "Shaq Interview: Dad and a Knicks Game Changed My Life Forever," YouTube, November 20, 2015, 6 min., 28 sec., www.youtube.com/watch?v=ZCXfzj1UEEg.

[2] The Book of Basketball, "San Antonio Spurs Tribute: The Beautiful Game," YouTube, July 20, 2014, 6 min., 20 sec., www.youtube.com/watch?v=T3y7cWmoBCI.

[3] "San Antonio Spurs," Statmuse, 2013-2014, www.statmuse.com/nba/team/san-antonio-spurs-27/2014.

[4] Robert Downen, Lise Olsen, and John Tedesco, "20 Years, 700 Victims: Southern Baptist Sexual Abuse Spreads as Leaders Resist Reforms," *Houston Chronicle*, February 10, 2019, www.houstonchronicle.com/news/investigations/article/Southern-Baptist-sexual-abuse-spreads-as-leaders-13588038.php; Wade Goodwyn, "Abuse by Boy Scout Leaders More Widespread than Earlier Thought," NPR, April 26, 2019, www.npr.org/2019/04/26/717201092/abuse-by-boy-scout-leaders-more-widespread-than-earlier-thought; U.S. Department of Justice, *Investigation of the Ferguson Police Department*, March 4, 2015, www.aclunc.org/sites/default/files/20150304-doj_report_on_ferguson.pdf; Martin Kaste, "DOJ Report Finds Systemic Patterns of Abuse by the Minneapolis Police Department," NPR, June 16, 2023, www.npr.org/2023/06/16/1182694978/doj-report-finds-systemic-patterns-of-abuse-by-the-minneapolis-police-department.

[5] For more on White American Folk Religion, see Jonathan Walton, "A Practical View of White American Christianity," KTF Press, June 16, 2022, www.ktfpress.com/p/a-practical-view-of-white-american.

[6] Roger Henderson, "Kuyper's Inch," *Pro Rege* 36, no. 3 (2008): 12-14. Available for download at https://digitalcollections.dordt.edu/pro_rege/vol36/iss3/2.

[7] "Poverty, Prosperity, and Planet Report," World Bank Group, 2024, www.world bank.org/en/publication/poverty-prosperity-and-planet.

[8] Anibal Quijano, "Coloniality and Modernity/Rationality," *Cultural Studies* 21, no. 2-3 (2007): 168-78.

[9] Lisa Lowe, *The Intimacies of Four Continents* (Durham, NC: Duke University Press, 2015).

5. REPEAT

[1] "COVID-19 Mortality by State," National Center for Health Statistics, Centers for Disease Control and Prevention, 2024, www.cdc.gov/nchs/pressroom/sosmap /covid19_mortality_final/COVID19.htm; "Queens County, New York Coronavirus Cases and Deaths," USAFacts, last updated July 2023, https://usafacts .org/visualizations/coronavirus-covid-19-spread-map/state/new-york/county /queens-county.

[2] Mind Tools Content Team, "Lewin's Force Field Analysis for Change Management," Change Management Insight, 2024, https://changemanagementinsight .com/lewins-force-field-analysis-change-management.

[3] Figure adapted from Mark Connelly, "Force Field Analysis—Kurt Lewin," Change Management Coach, updated May 1, 2023, www.change-management-coach .com/force-field-analysis.html.

[4] Noel Rae, "How Christian Slaveholders Used the Bible to Justify Slavery," *Time*, February 23, 2018, https://time.com/5171819/christianity-slavery-book-excerpt; Amanda Anderson, "The Great Evil: Christianity, the Bible, and the Native American Genocide," Pioneer PBS, September 2, 2022, www.pioneer.org/blogs/compass -stories/the-great-evil-christianity-the-bible-and-the-native-american-genocide; "The Dutch Reformed Church and Its Contribution to Apartheid," European Academy on Religion and Society, December 7, 2021, https://europeanacademyof religionandsociety.com/news/the-dutch-reformed-church-and-its-contribution -to-apartheid; Mimi Kirk, "Countering Christian Zionism in the Age of Trump," Middle East Research and Information Project (MERIP), August 8, 2019, https:// merip.org/2019/08/countering-christian-zionism-in-the-age-of-trump.

[5] "Mahatma Gandhi Says He Believes in Christ but not Christianity," *The Harvard Crimson*, January 11, 1927, https://archive.vn/X96mp.

[6] Benjamin Blaisdell and Ronda Taylor Bullock, "White Imagination, Black Reality: Recentering Critical Race Theory in Critical Whiteness Studies," *International Journal of Qualitative Studies in Education* 36, no. 8 (2023): 1450-58.

[7] Herbert Spencer, *Principles of Biology* (London: Williams and Norgate, 1864), 444.

[8] Jonathan P. Walton (@jonathanpanwalton), "What if we were all meant to be good Samaritans?" Instagram reel, April 16, 2024, www.instagram.com/reel /C50sU6pLrj4.

9 Peter Wohlleben, *The Hidden Life of Trees: What They Feel, How They Communicate—Discoveries from a Secret World*, trans. Jane Billinghurst (Vancouver, BC: Greystone Books, 2016).

10 Caroline Bologna, "Why the Phrase 'Pull Yourself Up by Your Bootstraps' Is Nonsense," HuffPost, June 12, 2018, www.huffpost.com/entry/pull-yourself-up-by -your-bootstraps-nonsense_n_5b1ed024e4b0bbb7a0e037d4.

11 I use the Peloton app every day to do at least one workout. With a busy schedule, it's an easy way to connect with my wife and friends as we hold each other accountable, share workouts, and so on. I get marked for being "active" even if I meditate. This not only keeps my weekly streak but reminds me that when I take time for silence I am making a conscious choice to "do" something. My all-time favorite podcast when the NBA season is in full swing is *The Mismatch* featuring Chris Vernon and Kevin O'Connor. When I was a kid, my brothers and I loved watching NBA basketball, and that endures today. Every week I wait for Josh Johnson's latest standup routine, and I love PBS's *Frontline* and National Geographic documentaries. My daily smoothie consists of two cups of almond milk, two tablespoons of peanut butter, two scoops of vegan protein powder, two tablespoons of cacao powder, and one large banana blended to perfection!

12 We started playing this game after a parenting workshop at our church and follow-up conversations in our small group Bible study. We were looking for ways to prioritize connection over correction for our kids, and I highly recommend it.

6. RECUPERATE

1 Naz Beheshti, "Toxic Influence: An Average of 80% of Americans Have Experienced Emotional Abuse," *Forbes*, May 15, 2020, www.forbes.com/sites /nazbeheshti/2020/05/15/an-average-of-80-of-americans-have-experienced -emotional-abuse.

2 Milena J. Wisniewska, "Domestic Violence Statistics 2024," Break the Cycle, last updated January 8, 2025, www.breakthecycle.org/domestic-violence-statistics.

3 Laura Fenton, "How to Grow a Bonsai Tree Indoors and Actually Keep It Alive," *Real Simple*, May 9, 2023, www.realsimple.com/home-organizing/gardening/indoor /how-to-grow-a-bonsai-tree-indoors-and-actually-keep-it-alive.

4 Natural Ways, "Grow Your Own Square Watermelons by Just Doing This," YouTube, September 13, 2017, 3 min., 9 sec., www.youtube.com/watch?v=iyqOcLIMMSI.

5 Robert Jones Jr., *The Prophets* (New York: G. P. Putnam's Sons, 2021), 301.

6 Christine Sarikas, "Vygotsky Scaffolding: What It Is and How to Use It," *PrepScholar Advice* (blog), last modified June 4, 2018, https://blog.prepscholar.com/vygotsky -scaffolding-zone-of-proximal-development.

7 Lauren Rubin and Dr. Lori Dassa, "Emotional Scaffolding and English Language Learners" (master's thesis, Florida Atlantic University, 2009), 10, https://fau.digital.flvc.org/islandora/object/fau%3A41560/datastream/OBJ/view /Emotional_Scaffolding_and_English_Language_Learners.pdf.

ABOUT THE AUTHOR

Jonathan Walton is a writer, speaker, and facilitator at the intersection of faith, justice, and emotional health. He leads Beauty and Resistance cohorts, writes *The Crux* on Substack, and is a senior resource specialist for InterVarsity Christian Fellowship focusing on political discipleship and civic engagement. He has written five books, including *Twelve Lies That Hold America Captive*. He holds a degree in creative writing from Columbia University and an MA from the City University in New York in the Study of the Americas. He lives in Queens, New York, with his wife and daughters and enjoys great food, almost every cooking show, and crying during Disney movies.

You can find him online at:

Substack: @jonathanwalton

Website: www.jonathan-walton.com

Instagram: @jonathanpanwalton

ALSO BY THE AUTHOR

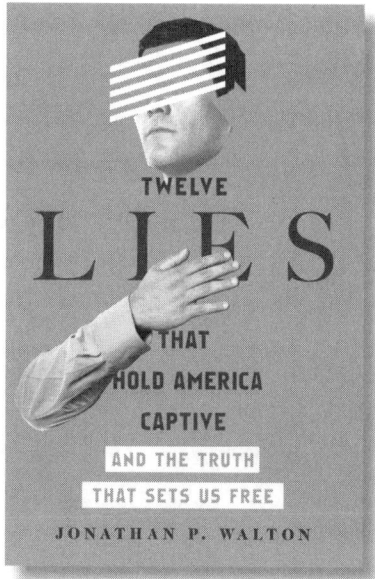

*Twelve Lies That Hold
America Captive*
978-0-8308-4558-3

Like this book?

Scan the code to discover more content like this!

Get on IVP's email list to receive special offers, exclusive book news, and thoughtful content from your favorite authors on topics you care about.

ivp | InterVarsity Press